"This is a heartfelt and courageous integration of psychological science and Christian faith. Dr. Knabb writes not only as a clinical psychologist and researcher but also as someone who's walked the hard road of trauma. This workbook will be a deeply helpful guide for Christians longing to move beyond rumination and into spiritual healing. I'm grateful this book exists."

Steven C. Hayes, *PhD, originator of acceptance and commitment therapy (ACT)*

"This is a very helpful, biblically based, psychologically sound, practical, and very well written workbook for Christian survivors of trauma. It clearly describes the four major Christian mental skills of attention, focus on the present moment, awareness, and acceptance for effectively shifting from trauma-based, unhelpful rumination to helpful rumination on God, one based on an explicitly Christian meditation on Scripture and prayer. Highly recommended!"

Siang-Yang Tan, *PhD, senior professor of clinical psychology, Fuller Theological Seminary, and author of Counseling and Psychotherapy: A Christian Perspective, 2nd ed*

"With remarkable vulnerability and clinical precision, Joshua Knabb brings together the best of trauma science and sacred Christian practice to help survivors face and heal from what most try to forget. His personal story, research, and empathy make this one of the most honest and hope-filled trauma resources available. Every counselor, pastor, and caregiver should keep this close for the clients they serve."

Tim Clinton, *EdD, LPC, LMFT, president, American Association of Christian Counselors*

"*The Christian Trauma Survivor's Workbook* combines best research-informed methods, clinical methods, and practical Christian wisdom (incorporating Scripture, thoughts from Puritans and wise Christians from the past, mindfulness, and meditation on Christian Scripture). It helps readers handle the challenges of trauma-based rumination—regardless of whether a person has been diagnosed with PTSD or has a few trauma symptoms. Joshua Knabb blends scientific insight, clinical understanding, and Christian wisdom. Every counselor and therapist will want to own this workbook and recommend it to patients."

Everett L. Worthington, Jr., *PhD, Commonwealth Professor emeritus, Virginia Commonwealth University*

"Based on a Christian worldview, grounded in a Christian theology of suffering, and well-informed by contemporary research on trauma and its healing, Dr. Knabb offers another excellent workbook, this time for Christians recovering from complex trauma. With its many references to the Bible and the Christian traditions, as well as contemporary mindfulness literature, those looking for a sound, evidence-based, Christian alternative to secular and Buddhist mindfulness approaches to trauma won't be disappointed."

Eric L. Johnson, *PhD, founder and scholar-in-residence,*
Christian Psychology Institute

"Many Christians wrestle with the lingering impact of trauma on their mental, emotional, and spiritual well-being. In *The Christian Trauma Survivor's Workbook*, Dr. Joshua Knabb thoughtfully integrates the latest psychological research on trauma treatment with a Christian worldview. The result is a practical, accessible, and compassionate resource for those seeking holistic healing."

Joshua N. Hook, *PhD, professor of counseling psychology and*
co-author of Thriving Families: A Trauma-Informed Guidebook for the
Foster and Adoptive Journey

"I can't recommend this workbook highly enough. With deep theological insight and clinical expertise, Dr. Joshua Knabb offers Christian trauma survivors a practical and hope-filled path for navigating trauma. This workbook weaves together psychological research and rich spiritual practices in a way that offers a comprehensive, evidence-informed approach to spiritual and emotional healing. A deeply needed, must-read practical resource for anyone walking alongside others impacted by trauma."

Jamie Aten, *PhD, founder of the Humanitarian Disaster Institute at*
Wheaton College and co-founder of Spiritual First Aid

"A thoughtful, thorough, practical, and skills-based resource to support the recovery process of trauma survivors. I appreciated how conversant the discussion was not only to recent research, but also to the riches of historical Christian spiritual and meditative practices. There is a dearth of resources and literature that take seriously the disruptive impact of trauma upon one's spiritual life and worldview, and I believe this work helps address this gap."

David C. Wang, *ThM, PhD, Cliff and Joyce Penner Chair for the*
Formation of Emotionally Healthy Leaders, Fuller Theological Seminary

THE CHRISTIAN TRAUMA
Survivor's Workbook

The Christian Trauma Survivor's Workbook is a step-by-step guide for supporting Christians who have a history of trauma. The workbook offers four research-supported skills—attention, focus on the present moment, awareness, and acceptance—to help Christians shift from trauma-based patterns of ruminative thinking that can keep them stuck and make trauma symptoms worse to focusing on God. Drawing on Christian meditative prayer and contemplative practices that are anchored to the Bible and Christian spiritual writings, chapters include useful definitions, explanations, step-by-step interventions with audio files, journaling exercises, and real-life examples.

Joshua J. Knabb is a board-certified clinical psychologist and licensed minister. He is associate dean for the psychology division and director of the PsyD program in the College of Behavioral and Social Sciences at California Baptist University.

THE CHRISTIAN TRAUMA
Survivor's Workbook

A Skills-Based Approach for Psychological and Spiritual Healing

Joshua J. Knabb

Routledge
Taylor & Francis Group

NEW YORK AND LONDON

Designed cover image: Getty Images

First published 2026
by Routledge
605 Third Avenue, New York, NY 10158

and by Routledge
4 Park Square, Milton Park, Abingdon, Oxon, OX14 4RN

Routledge is an imprint of the Taylor & Francis Group, an informa business

© 2026 Joshua J. Knabb

For Product Safety Concerns and Information please contact our EU representative GPSR@taylorandfrancis.com. Taylor & Francis Verlag GmbH, Kaufingerstraße 24, 80331 München, Germany.

ISBN: 9781041088615 (hbk)
ISBN: 9781041088608 (pbk)
ISBN: 9781003647270 (ebk)

DOI: 10.4324/9781003647270

Typeset in Warnock Pro
by Newgen Publishing UK

Access the Support Material: www.routledge.com/9781041088608

This book is dedicated to my wonderful wife, Adrienne, and children, Emory and Rowan, who help me to heal on a daily basis from the lingering trauma I first experienced as an adolescent.

Contents

Contents

About the Author

Joshua J. Knabb, PsyD, ABPP, is a board-certified clinical psychologist with the American Board of Professional Psychology and fellow of the American Academy of Clinical Psychology, specializing in individual and couples therapy. Residing in Southern California with his wife and two children, Dr. Knabb is a tenured professor of psychology at California Baptist University (CBU), serving as the associate dean for the Psychology Division and director of the Doctor of Psychology (PsyD) in Clinical Psychology program in the College of Behavioral and Social Sciences. In addition to his work as an educator and psychotherapist, Dr. Knabb is the editor for the *Journal of Psychology and Christianity*, and his writings and research have been published in a wide variety of academic journals, textbooks, and workbooks over the last 15 years. His research interests include marriage and the family, psychological assessment, attachment theory, transdiagnostic constructs and interventions, mindfulness-based therapies, the psychology of religion and spirituality, Christian meditative and contemplative practices, and cultural diversity. Finally, Dr. Knabb is a licensed minister, serving at the Palm Avenue Campus of Sandals Church in Riverside, California.

Acknowledgments

First, I'd like to thank my amazing wife, Adrienne, who provided me with incredible support as I wrote this workbook and helpful editorial feedback on multiple chapters. Second, I'd like to recognize Anna Moore at Routledge for supporting the publication of this workbook. Third, I'd like to acknowledge my co-researchers from the original research projects that served as the empirical foundation for this workbook: Veola Vazquez, Robert Pate, Fernando Garzon, Kenneth Wang, DeAndra Edison-Riley, Alexandra Slick, Roy'Alle Smith, and Sarah Weber. Lastly, I'd like to thank God, who offers comfort and peace in the midst of psychological suffering.

Permissions

CHAPTER 1

Introduction

I can still remember the evening with stark, devastating clarity. I had just learned from my mother that my father was moving out the very next morning. At the time, my father was somewhat heavyset and stood at just under six feet tall with a graying beard, strawberry blonde hair, and inquisitive light blue eyes hiding behind large-rimmed glasses with thick lenses. Although he looked innocent, he was on the verge of causing me a lifetime of psychological pain. Despite the gravity of the realization, I was still woefully unprepared for the change that was yet to come. "Your father is seeing someone else and has decided to move out," she reluctantly shared with a discouraged and disparaging tone I had never heard from her before.

On this fateful night over three decades ago, my father was in his early 40s. He was seemingly going through a "midlife crisis," something all too familiar to many middle-class families in the United States, both then and now. Married to my mother for some 15 years as a first-generation Christian, he had been in an extramarital romantic relationship for months, if not years, with a coworker about 15 years his junior. Sharing a tiny office with this female colleague, they had begun the affair shortly after developing a close working relationship. This was unbeknownst to me as I confidently and ignorantly trekked toward adolescence.

Against the backdrop of a buzzing silence that permeated the house, I didn't know what to do. I felt a devastating sense of powerlessness and panic, coupled with overwhelming sadness and shame. Sadness for the irreplicable loss that was going to occur the next morning. And shame because I blamed myself for my father's decision to leave. "If only he loved me more, he would stay," I thought to myself. I truly struggled to understand how a man who had raised his family to follow Christ could make such a worldview-shattering

DOI: 10.4324/9781003647270-1

decision. He seemed to be prioritizing himself, and himself alone, above his Lord, wife, and two sons.

As my father laid in his bed upstairs that evening watching television—appearing stoic, emotionless, and mummy-like—I slouched down as far as I could in a gray, round, velvet swivel chair downstairs. I sat in that dark room alone and pleaded for him to stay. "Please don't go. I need you. I can't survive without you. You'll ruin my life." For what seemed like an eternity, I yelled some combination of these desperate pleas to my father who remained unresponsive and unmoved. Frantically swiveling back and forth, my body no longer able to contain the rising panic, I tried to convince my unsympathetic father to stay. I can remember feeling abandoned, alone, and betrayed. For the first time in my short life, I was faced with an array of traumatic emotions because of my father's silence and abandonment. I was totally dysregulated, overwhelmed, and alone.

With no real response from a father who now resembled more of a stranger than the spiritual leader of our home, I can still recall the penetrating fear that permeated my entire being. I was unsure of how to make sense of this now scary, unpredictable, and threatening world and my place in it. I can also remember the deep shame I felt at the core of my being in not believing I was good enough for him to stay. The sadness was unbearable, given my whole world was cracking and crumbling before my eyes. There was no proverbial glue to piece back together the shards of my now shattered reality.

It's true that many children in Western societies are impacted by the fallout of divorce. Why, then, was the divorce of my parents so traumatizing for *me*? My parents were up to this point devout first-generation Christians. They gave their lives to Christ in college, where they met and fell in love. Over the next decade and a half, they would display their love for Jesus in a variety of admirable ways. They volunteered in prison ministries to share the gospel message, traveled overseas for missionary work, and served on staff with various churches. They raised my twin brother and I to prioritize God above *all* else, teaching us about the need for Christ in every area of our lives. All the while, they were committed to biblical orthodoxy.

Out of this childhood experience emerged a coherent and guiding Christian worldview, a comprehensive way of understanding reality. I increasingly used this view of the world to make sense of life. As I observed school friends struggle with their parents' divorce from a distance, I felt secure in knowing this type of tragedy would never happen to me. I was seemingly protected from the proverbial storms of life, given my parents fervently followed Jesus and his teachings. It was as if their faith in Christ gave me an unrealistic faith in their invincibility as my parents.

These early experiences have left me deeply traumatized for years. I've been filled with an overwhelming array of distressing emotions like sadness, fear, anxiety, shame, and anger. I've repeatedly asked spiritual questions of unrelenting doubt, such as "Why did you let this happen, God?" and "God, will this happen to me in my own marriage?" I've struggled with a sense that relationships, with both God and others, are unsafe, unpredictable, uncertain, and even dangerous. I've experienced a significant change in how I see the world, referred to as a "shattered worldview" in trauma research.[1] And I've struggled with vivid memories of my father ignoring my panicked pleas for him to stay.

Despite my current age, the many decades that have passed, and my father's eventual passing from terminal cancer in my mid-20s, these events continue to have a significant impact on me. On any given day, I may experience painful memories and overwhelming emotions. I may compulsively ask questions regarding God's role or lack thereof in my parents' divorce. Worst of all, I struggle with whether it will happen in my own marriage.

Although I wanted nothing more than for my father to come home, trauma moved in instead. With no choice but to move forward, I've learned to endure this trauma as an unruly house guest with an extended stay. As part of this growth process, I've developed a pattern of gently shifting from ruminating about my father's absence and the pain he caused to ruminating on God's Word, the Bible. Earthly rumination rarely provides me with answers. Rather, it leaves me stuck and distracted. This pivot,[2] or shift in both perspective and focus, I've learned has provided me with peace, comfort, and the ability to endure continued suffering. Although my trauma-related suffering may never fully go away on this side of heaven, I've discovered a practical strategy to better manage it.

It's as if I come to a mental fork in the road every time I struggle with unwanted intrusive memories and distressing emotions, which I'll be unpacking in more detail in this workbook. I can travel alone down the road of unhelpful rumination, which makes my symptoms worse and leaves me tired and isolated. Or I can head down the road of helpful rumination, choosing to focus on and journey with the God of love.[3] I'm always traveling down a road, like I'm always thinking, pondering, dwelling, meditating, and ruminating on something. Because of this, I need to be intentional about which road I choose to travel down. If rumination is simply defined as repetitive thought, I can ruminate as an avoidance strategy,[4] which does not lead to the intended eradication of emotional pain. Or I can ruminate as a growth strategy, focusing on the God of love who understands my suffering and soothes and comforts my emotional pain. And I need to switch roads when I notice I'm traveling down the wrong one. This switch is most significant when the busyness of an overactive mind begins to dominate my inner world and talk me out of my confidence in and walk with Christ.

Traumatic Events, Trauma, and Secular Psychology

As the above example poignantly reveals, there are many types of traumatic events that can lead to an intense and distressing trauma response. This psychological response may be enduring and far-reaching and impact family life, work life, and religious life. Some traumatic events involve actual threats to our immediate personal safety, such as physical, intimate/domestic partner, or sexual violence.[5] Other traumatic events consist of witnessing a loved one's death, an accident (such as a natural disaster or car crash), or violence inflicted on someone else.[6] One survey found that three-fourths of adults reported experiencing a traumatic event in their lifetime, such as observing someone else being severely hurt or killed or experiencing someone else dying.[7]

Psychological responses to these traumatic events, called trauma or trauma symptoms, can be devastating and interfere with daily life. We may experience a range of difficult psychological reactions like unpleasant thoughts, feelings, sensations, memories, and images. We might begin to believe the world is unsafe and even find evidence to support this assumption. These symptoms can fall into one of four main categories. First, someone may struggle with intrusive, distressing, and vivid memories, dreams, or flashbacks of the traumatic event within the inner world. Second, an individual may avoid reminders of the traumatic event in the outer world, such as the scene of a crime or conversations about the event. Third, a trauma survivor may suffer from difficult thoughts such as "I'm worthless," "It's my fault," or "The world is unsafe" and emotions including fear, anxiety, anger, helplessness, guilt, and shame related to the traumatic event. Finally, someone might experience extreme sensitivity and arousal such as trouble concentrating or being easily startled by noise in response to the traumatic event.[8]

What makes traumatic events so difficult, leading to a trauma response of psychological suffering, is that they create doubt that wasn't there before. Prior to the event, we may have believed that we have control and power in our daily life. We may have also believed that the world is consistent, safe, and trustworthy. Finally, we may have believed that the world is fair, just, and moral, with "good guys" succeeding and "bad guys" being punished. These beliefs about a "just, safe, and predictable"[9] world may crumble when we experience a traumatic event. This "worldview shattering"[10] experience can lead to more enduring symptoms of rumination, worry, uncertainty, doubt, fear, anxiety, cautiousness, and withdrawal, which make daily life much more difficult.

When these symptoms are experienced over time and prevent us from functioning in life, they may lead to a formal diagnosis of posttraumatic stress disorder (PTSD). This clinical diagnosis is captured in the *Diagnostic and*

Statistical Manual of Mental Disorders, which is now in a text-revised fifth edition (DSM-5-TR).[11] Still, since only around one in ten adults are diagnosed with PTSD, many trauma survivors will suffer *some* symptoms without being formally diagnosed.[12] And some non-DSM-5-TR trauma symptoms may be experienced either alongside or without a formal PTSD diagnosis.

One such symptom is trauma-based rumination, which involves thinking repeatedly in a perseverative and repetitive manner about the meaning of the event, the causes and consequences of the event, or our emotional response to the event.[13] This type of rumination can often be counterproductive since it may keep us focused on what led up to the event and what happened after the event rather than being able to actually process, in a healthy and accurate way, memories of the event and how we felt (and still feel) about it.[14] Rumination may also distract us from life because we are "lost in our head." And, unfortunately, it may lead to no real resolution. Without a formal diagnosis, the individual experiencing such ruminative thoughts may not recognize them as a trauma response.

Unhelpful forms of rumination can be sort of like riding a carousel. As a kid, I can remember riding one every so often. After about a minute or so, it became apparent that riding the fiberglass horse didn't get me anywhere. Instead, I just went around and around in a passive manner. Unlike riding a real horse toward a real destination in an active manner, I never moved forward. Likewise, unhelpful types of rumination can be like passively riding a carousel. We go over and over the material in our mind as we think in circles. We never get where we want to go—obtaining satisfying answers and resolving the issue at hand. This is where trauma-based rumination comes into play when considering a range of trauma symptoms.

One understanding of trauma[15] suggests that, following a traumatic event, we may end up experiencing regular intrusive memories of the incident. These are vivid and lifelike, and they may lead to added suffering. Upon experiencing these memories that seem like they are truly happening in the here-and-now, we may struggle with distressing and unwanted emotional reactions such as fear, anxiety, anger, helplessness, guilt, or shame. In response to these emotions, we may end up compulsively ruminating to avoid both the memories and emotions. Rumination is about dwelling on abstract thoughts so that we don't have to feel concrete emotions. These ruminations might consist of repeatedly asking "Why" ("Why did this happen to me?") and "What if" ("What if it happens again?") questions about the event in a passive manner. This type of rumination is passive and unhelpful because we never really get anywhere. We never answer the questions we are repeating to ourselves, solve our problems, or grow. Rather, we may use our ruminative thoughts to avoid our emotions, which leaves us stuck. We may dwell on the causes and consequences of the event but not process, in a healthy manner, how we felt and feel about what happened. When we ruminate in this unproductive way, we might intensify the very memories and emotions we are hoping to avoid.

To address this dilemma, some researchers have developed strategies for being more accepting of trauma-related memories and emotions. This contrasts with getting stuck in unhelpful and passive patterns of rumination that may make things worse. Collectively called mindfulness, many clinical psychologists advocate for a distinct set of mental skills—attention, focus on the present moment, awareness, and acceptance—to relate differently to our difficult thoughts, feelings, sensations, memories, and images.[16] These unique skills[17] include attention, which consists of focusing on one thing at a time in a sustained manner rather than the mind being divided. Another skill is staying rooted in the present moment not preoccupied with the past or future. Awareness, moreover, is an important skill. It involves being fully alert to whatever emerges in the inner world, not distracted. Finally, the skill of acceptance consists of embracing, rather than avoiding, all our inner experiences. Research has found that mindfulness is negatively related to rumination.[18] This means that the more people report practicing mindfulness, the less they report ruminating. A recent review of just over 60 studies on mindfulness as an intervention for rumination found that it is helpful for reducing ruminative thinking.[19]

This understanding of the problem of and solution to trauma symptoms often comes to us from cognitive behavioral therapy (CBT) in clinical psychology. With CBT, psychologists help clients to better understand the relationship between thoughts, feelings, and behaviors to make positive changes in life. According to CBT, it is our interpretation of what happens to us (our thoughts), not what actually happens (the events of life), that better determines how we will feel (our emotions) and what we will do (our behaviors) moving forward.[20] For instance, my optimistic interpretation of a job loss as providing me with an opportunity for a positive career change, not the job loss itself, may better determine whether I develop depressive or anxiety symptoms. There is some debate, though, within CBT about whether we should try to change our thoughts when they are not accurate or reflective of reality or simply accept them as mere thinking like with mindfulness. "I need to change this distorted thought" versus "It's just a thought."[21]

As a quick example, we may originally have been the victim of a violent assault. In turn, we might think to ourselves "I'm going to be assaulted again" whenever we are walking in public and hear a sound behind us. With some forms of CBT, we may work with a psychologist to directly dispute the thought and replace it. We may label it as a category of distorted thinking known as "fortune telling," or predicting the future in negative ways without evidence, given we don't have a crystal ball to see what's ahead.[22] We may then change it to something like, "Although I was assaulted in the past, I'm safe right now." This is a direct method to change our thinking head on. With mindfulness, though, rather than directly disputing and replacing distorted thoughts, we simply notice them with non-judgment and allow them to run their natural course. This is an indirect method because we don't try to change the thought head on. We recognize that it's merely a thought without needing to do anything with it. From there, we can focus on something else in our awareness, like one of our senses (sight, sound, taste, touch, smell) or breathing.

I believe accepting our thoughts with non-judgment is optimal, not disputing and replacing them. This is because with disputing and replacing, we may end up spending all our time and mental energy trying to get rid of thoughts that will never fully go away. These efforts to avoid our thoughts are both exhausting and distracting. Instead, I believe it is better to make peace with our thoughts and see them from a bit more distance. For example, as a chronic worrier, I've developed the habit of noticing when I'm worrying from a place of openness and curiosity with a simple statement, "I'm worrying again," without needing to change the worry or judge myself for it. We can learn to view thoughts as mere thoughts that don't have to determine what we do in life. I prefer *indirectly* dealing with difficult thoughts such as noticing thoughts and gently shifting toward something else to focus on. This is contrasted with *directly* dealing with them by trying to change or eliminate them. With rumination, we can learn to notice it, then flexibly pivot toward something else. (For Christians, we can ruminate on God and God's Word, the Bible.)

Because mindfulness—even seemingly secularized/non-religious versions used within CBT—originally comes to us from the Buddhist religious tradition,[23] some Christians may have concerns about drawing upon another religious heritage for insights into the mind and healthy psychological functioning. Throughout this workbook, thus, I will be turning to Christianity's spiritual practices, including prayer and meditation. These can help us develop the similar requisite mental skills of attention, focus on the present moment, awareness, and acceptance as in mindfulness.[24] These practices, however, have a much different purpose than with mindfulness. Their purpose is to deepen our relationship with God, with the amelioration of suffering as a possible byproduct. This Christian aim is contrasted with simply helping us understand and eradicate suffering, as is commonly the case with Buddhist-derived mindfulness.[25] Christian spiritual practices are relational and point us to God as our source of inner peace and comfort. On the other hand, Buddhist practices like mindfulness are individualized and direct us to the self as the change agent. Many of these similarities and distinctions will be discussed in greater detail throughout the workbook.

Nevertheless, my hope is that this workbook, drawing upon many of these insights from psychological science, can help you learn to shift from unhelpful trauma-based rumination to more helpful strategies for managing intrusive memories and corresponding distressing emotions. If rumination doesn't work in the long run, we need another approach for responding to trauma-related memories and emotions. We'll unpack this skill-based strategy together. Let's now examine trauma in the context of the Christian tradition.

Traumatic Events, Trauma, and Christianity

For Christian trauma survivors, there may be additional considerations such as uniquely Christian forms of rumination. For example, we may compulsively ask "Why" and "What if" questions in the context of our relationship with the Triune God of the Bible. These may include "Why did you allow this to happen, Father?" or "Jesus, what if you turn away from me when this happens again?" (This has certainly been my own experience, given I regularly and painfully lamented to God after my earthly father left. I questioned how God could allow such a tragedy to occur so early on in my life.) So, we need to also consider our own faith tradition, including a personal relationship with God and God's Word, the Bible, when making sense of traumatic events and our responses to them.

Within the roughly 2,000-year-old Christian religious tradition, we have prayer and meditation practices[26] not Buddhist-derived mindfulness. These practices have been handed down to us from our Christian ancestors for the purpose of deepening our relationship with God and better managing psychological and spiritual suffering. When practiced, prayer and meditation can help us develop the mental skills of attention, focus on the present moment, awareness, and acceptance.[27] However, the steps to practice historic Christian spiritual exercises are different from mindfulness. Also, their ultimate purpose, or *telos*, is different from Buddhist mindfulness. For Christians, these practices help us to commune or fellowship with the Triune God. Mindfulness, on the other hand, is used to gain insight into a Buddhist understanding of reality—there is no individual self, life is suffering, and everything is impermanent—collectively called the "three marks of existence." Buddhist practices involve letting go of any notion of a fixed sense of self and sense of permanence to eradicate suffering, whereas Christian practices focus on developing a deeper relationship with God as *the* source of all comfort and understanding.

With Christian prayer, which Jesus taught his disciples in the gospels,[28] we are using our thoughts to spend time and communicate with God. We can praise God, petition God for help, and confess sin to God, among other prayer themes. Like prayer, Christian meditation involves employing our thoughts and reasoning to relate to God. Yet, we are often pondering and ruminating on God and God's Word on a much deeper level with meditation than with prayer. In either case, with both prayer and meditation we are shifting our focus from earthly preoccupations such as rumination to God. As we focus on God, we may consider his attributes/characteristics like his infinite love and goodness. We may also meditate on his actions such as his protection or guiding care. Focusing on God's promises to us in Scripture, moreover, is a theme for Christian meditation.

Within our centuries-old Christian religious heritage, there are many different "streams" of Christian psychological and spiritual traditions and prayer and meditative practices that flow from the three main branches of Christianity—Catholic, Orthodox, and Protestant.[29] I will be drawing from several of these traditions to help you, as a Christian trauma survivor, relate differently to trauma-based rumination via the mental skills of attention, focus on the present moment, awareness, and acceptance.[30]

As one example, the Puritans were Protestants from England in the 1500s and 1600s who wrote extensively on biblical meditation.[31] I believe biblical meditation can be key for developing focused and sustained attention to shift from unhelpful rumination to God. As a second example, Brother Lawrence, a humble Catholic monk, wrote in the 1600s on a spiritual strategy for practicing God's presence in all of life. This practice can be helpful to stay anchored to the here-and-now, where God is with us and ministering to us, not lost in rumination about past traumatic events. As a third example, the Orthodox Church draws inspiration from the *Philokalia*, a collection of monastic spiritual writings spanning the 4th to 15th centuries, to practice the Jesus Prayer. The shorter form of this famous prayer is "Lord Jesus Christ, have mercy on me." I believe this type of prayer can be helpful to cultivate awareness of the inner world. We can notice rumination then gently shift to the words of the prayer. As a fourth and final example, the Jesuit tradition within Catholicism advocates for the use of the daily examen. This exercise is derived from the 16th century work, *Spiritual Exercises*, as a prayer practice to accept God's presence throughout the day. This practice can also be helpful in learning to make peace with the inner world including trauma-based memories, emotions, and rumination. As we learn to accept our inner world, we can invite God to be with us throughout the day and recognize his presence in our psychological struggles.

With the help of several colleagues, I have drawn on these four Christian sources to research trauma-related rumination and its interventions from a Christian perspective. This line of research includes what happens psychologically and spiritually in response to traumatic events and how we can draw upon our own religious tradition to ameliorate trauma symptoms. Based on two published empirical studies, I found that Christians can learn to shift from unhelpful rumination to helpful rumination with a purpose, which may reduce trauma symptoms.[32] This intentional shift can occur when Christians draw upon the aforementioned spiritual practices within the centuries-old Christian tradition to cultivate the skills of attention, focus on the present moment,

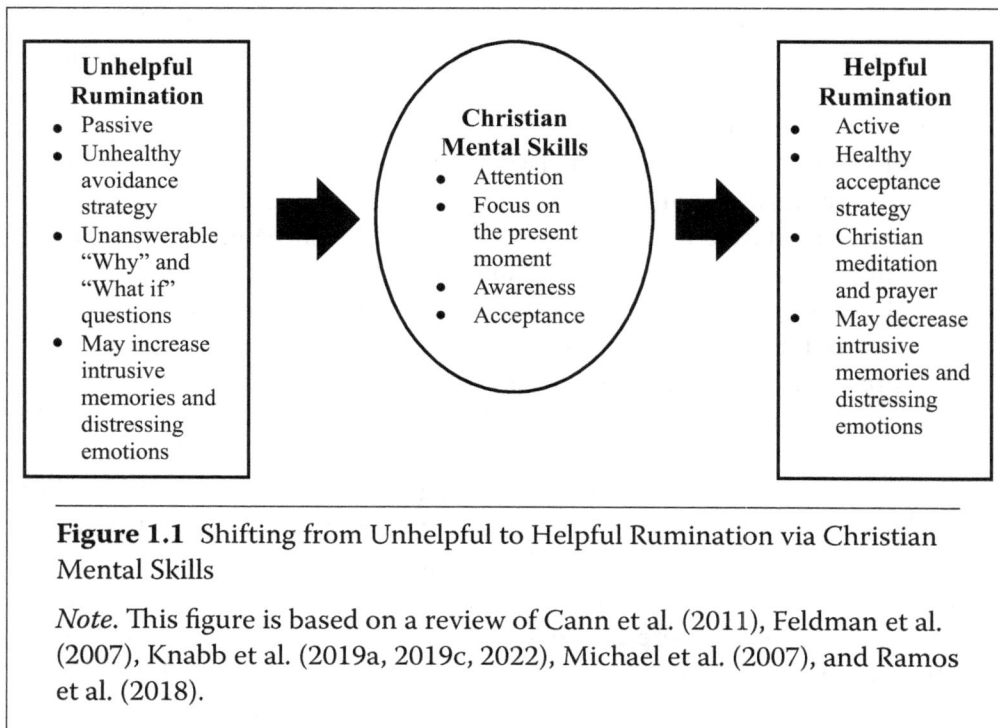

Figure 1.1 Shifting from Unhelpful to Helpful Rumination via Christian Mental Skills

Note. This figure is based on a review of Cann et al. (2011), Feldman et al. (2007), Knabb et al. (2019a, 2019c, 2022), Michael et al. (2007), and Ramos et al. (2018).

awareness, and acceptance.[33] This, again, is the focus of the workbook. See Figure 1.1 for a visual depiction of this important process in action. Prior to concluding this chapter, I'd like to present the purpose, contents, and theme of the workbook before you.

The Purpose, Contents, and Theme of This Workbook

This workbook is based on my own life experiences, professional training, and original research on trauma-based rumination from a Christian perspective. It was written for Christian trauma survivors to learn a different way to respond to trauma-based intrusive memories beyond getting stuck in unhelpful forms of rumination. The workbook can be used as a standalone resource for Christian trauma survivors, in church settings, or as a supplement to professional counseling or psychotherapy. Each chapter contains explanations and exercises to learn a new way of responding to trauma symptoms, doing so from a Christian perspective. As a trauma survivor myself, board-certified clinical psychologist, behavioral scientist, and, most importantly, committed Christ follower, I want to be a part of your experience through this process. This workbook, however, is not meant to take the place of psychotherapy or professional counseling. If your overall functioning is impaired and you are unable to carry out daily activities, please make an appointment to see a mental health professional.

Throughout the workbook, I write from a Reformed Protestant perspective. This includes the application of Scripture to all of life, belief in Jesus Christ alone to repair the rupture between humankind and God and for salvation, and the unwavering recognition that God is infinitely loving, powerful, wise, present, and holy. Even when I draw upon Catholic and Orthodox sources outside of Protestant Christianity, I interpret them "evangelically."[34] This means I still return to my Reformed Protestant roots to make sense of them. However, because my humble aim is to begin and end with the Bible and a biblical view of the world, my hope is that all Christians—whether Catholic, Orthodox, or Protestant—can benefit from this workbook. With Christianity as my foundation, I also draw upon recent insights from trauma research within the scientific discipline of psychology. We'll unpack this more in the pages that follow.

In the second chapter, I review a secular psychological perspective on trauma. This is followed by a Christian understanding in the third chapter. With the fourth chapter, I introduce the background, theme, and goals for the four-skill integrative approach for shifting from unhelpful to helpful[35] forms of rumination to assist you in better managing your trauma symptoms. In this approach, I draw upon insights from psychological science and a CBT perspective on trauma and its interventions. I also cite Scripture, Puritan writings on God's promises, Brother Lawrence's *The Practice of the Presence of God*, Orthodox writings on the Jesus Prayer, and Jesuit writings on the daily exam, all within the Christian tradition.[36] The fifth through eighth chapters focus on each of the four mental skills needed to make this important shift including attention, focus on the present moment, awareness, and acceptance.[37] Chapter 5 emphasizes the skill of Christian attention, which is revealed throughout Scripture and practiced via Puritan meditation. Chapter 6 focuses on the skill of Christian focus on the present moment, which is anchored to Bother Lawrence's writings on practicing God's presence in the here-and-now. Chapter 7 uses the skill of Christian awareness, which is practiced by way of the centuries-old Jesus Prayer. As the concluding chapter, Chapter 8 explores the skill of Christian acceptance, which is practiced vis-à-vis the Jesuit exercise of the daily examen. Within these four skill-based chapters, I offer explanations, exercises, journaling, and real-world examples (many clinical) for you to better understand and apply the material.

My prayer is that this workbook will help you as a Christian trauma survivor to, empowered by the Holy Spirit, more confidently walk with the Son home to the outstretched arms of the Father. I believe this Trinitarian understanding of the Christian life fittingly captures Christian mental health. My hope is that we can travel together to, with the help of the God of the Bible, pivot from getting stuck compulsively asking "Why" and "What if" questions to focusing on who God has revealed himself to be within Scripture. With God's Word, the Bible, as our beginning and ending point, we will draw upon our Christian tradition as well as psychological science to impact positive change. And we will walk with God each step of the way. Inspired by the Apostle Paul's instructions to "set [our] minds on things above,"[38] we will work toward shifting from earthly preoccupations like rumination to ruminating on the God who offers us peace amid suffering on this side of heaven.[39]

Concluding Exercise

Before ending this introduction chapter, attempt to come up with three goals for yourself as you undertake this shift in perspective. Try to develop goals that are *MAPS*.[40] This means they are, first, *measurable*, and you can track them over time ("I will practice the skills in this workbook twice per day"). Second, they should be *attainable*, meaning you can realistically achieve them ("I will read this workbook three days a week for the next month"). Third, they should be *positive* via focusing on what you *will* do rather than *won't* do ("I will meditate on God's promises in the Bible at least once per day," not "I won't ruminate"). Finally, they should be *specific* and detailed enough to know whether you are achieving them, not vague ("I will practice the Jesus Prayer for 20 minutes each day in a quiet environment to fellowship with God," not "I will practice as often as possible"). Please use extra paper if needed.

1. _____.

2. _____.

3. _____.

Notes

1 Gluhoski and Wortman (1996).
2 Throughout this workbook, I use the word "pivot," which is inspired by the work of Steve Hayes and acceptance and commitment therapy (ACT; see Hayes, 2019).
3 Knabb (2022).
4 Ramos et al. (2018).
5 APA Dictionary (n.d.f); Kessler et al. (2017).
6 APA Dictionary (n.d.f); Kessler et al. (2017).
7 Mills et al. (2011).
8 APA (2022).

 9 APA Dictionary (n.d.f).
10 Gluhoski and Wortman (1996).
11 APA (2022).
12 Atwoli et al. (2015).
13 Ehlers and Clark (2000); Moulds et al. (2020).
14 Ehlers and Clark (2000).
15 This paragraph is based on theory and research from Bishop et al. (2018); Ehlers and Clark (2000); Ehring and Ehlers (2014); Michael et al. (2007); and Ramos et al. (2018).
16 Feldman et al. (2007).
17 Feldman et al. (2007).
18 Knabb et al. (2019a).
19 Mao et al. (2023).
20 Beck (2021).
21 Hayes et al. (2011).
22 Leahy (2017).
23 Tirch et al. (2016).
24 Feldman et al. (2007).
25 Tirch et al. (2016).
26 In this paragraph and the next, the content is based on a review of the dictionary entries on prayer, meditation, and contemplation in *The Upper Room Dictionary of Christian Spiritual Formation* (Beasley-Topliffe, 2003).
27 Knabb et al. (2022).
28 Matthew 6:9–13.
29 Foster (2001).
30 Feldman et al. (2007).
31 See Beeke (2016).
32 Knabb et al. (2019a, 2022); see also Cann et al. (2011).
33 Feldman et al. (2007); Knabb et al. (2019a, 2019c, 2022).
34 Goggin and Strobel (2013).
35 Cann et al. (2011).
36 Knabb et al. (2019c).
37 Feldman et al. (2007); Knabb et al. (2019c).
38 Colossians 3:2.
39 John 16:33.
40 Chang et al. (2013).

CHAPTER 2

Trauma

A Secular Psychological Perspective

Introduction

In the second chapter, we'll review the different types of traumatic events that people tragically, yet commonly, experience in contemporary society. In turn, we'll discuss the different types of trauma symptoms that trauma survivors may experience. This includes the symptoms that lead to a formal diagnosis of posttraumatic stress disorder (PTSD) and non-DSM-5-TR symptoms like trauma-based rumination. After we cover the symptoms of trauma, we'll explore different interventions for trauma-related symptoms and disorders. We'll especially focus on cognitive behavioral therapy (CBT) interventions such as prolonged exposure and mindfulness-based approaches. Throughout the chapter, I'll offer definitions, explanations, exercises, and real-life examples to help you better understand traumatic events and trauma-based symptoms, disorders, and interventions from a secular psychological perspective.

Traumatic Events

In contemporary society, exposure to a traumatic event is commonplace. In a survey of almost 70,000 individuals from 24 countries and six continents, over two-thirds reported experiencing one or more traumatic events.[1] Among all survey respondents, close to one-third reported at least four traumatic events. Results revealed that there were five kinds of traumatic events that made up most of the reported events. These types included "witnessing death or serious injury, the unexpected death of a loved one, being mugged, being in a life-threatening automobile accident, and experiencing a life-threatening illness or injury."[2] From these results, we can see that experiencing a traumatic event is quite frequent worldwide. We can also ascertain that the types of events

DOI: 10.4324/9781003647270-2

can vary from a near-death experience we experience personally, to a physical threat to our own immediate safety, to witnessing a traumatic event being inflicted on someone else.

In addition to these types of more general survey-based studies of traumatic events, researchers have more narrowly examined what are called "adverse childhood experiences," or ACEs. These early experiences in life can be traumatizing and have a long-term psychological impact on children that extends well into adulthood. In the late 1990s, researchers defined ACEs as "childhood abuse and household dysfunction during childhood."[3] Originally, an ACEs survey was sent out to over 13,000 adults, with almost 10,000 responding to the survey.[4] Within the survey, the adults were asked about seven types of childhood adversities: "psychological, physical, or sexual abuse; violence against [their] mother; or living with household members who were substance abusers, mentally ill or suicidal, or ever imprisoned." Here, we can see that ACEs range from *personally experiencing* being insulted, hit, slapped, shoved, or sexually abused by a parent or caregiver to *witnessing* a parent or caregiver struggle with drug or alcohol addiction, a mental illness, or domestic violence.[5] Survey results revealed that over 50% of those who completed the questionnaire indicated they experienced at least one of the ACEs, with around 25% stating they experienced two or more ACEs. For individuals who endorsed suffering from at least four ACEs, they also reported a greater likelihood of currently struggling with a range of psychological issues when compared to the adults who disclosed no ACEs. These struggles in adulthood included alcohol and drug problems, depression, and attempted suicide. This pioneering study suggests that most adults in the U.S. may have suffered from traumatic events in childhood. These events, in turn, may lead to psychological vulnerabilities in adulthood, well after the childhood events took place. Such struggles may include the development of trauma-related symptoms and disorders,[6] described next.

Trauma Symptoms

Posttraumatic Stress Disorder (PTSD)

For individuals who experience one or more traumatic events in life, we may go on to suffer from psychological symptoms, which are called trauma or trauma symptoms (briefly introduced in Chapter 1). Based on the number of symptoms, how long they are experienced, and whether they prevent us from living life determines whether a formal psychiatric diagnosis is warranted.

Within the *Diagnostic and Statistical Manual of Mental Disorders*, currently published as a text-revised fifth edition (DSM-5-TR) by the American Psychiatric Association (2022), PTSD involves either personally experiencing or witnessing "actual or threatened death, serious injury, or sexual violence."[7] In response to these types of serious traumatic events, psychological symptoms may develop across four main categories.

First, we may suffer from intrusive symptoms, such as memories, dreams, or flashbacks of the event. For example, after a near-death car accident that involved Adam violently smashing his pickup truck into a larger delivery vehicle on the freeway during stop-and-go traffic, he continued to struggle with vivid memories of the event over a month after it happened. Driving home from work several weeks after the event, he would be overwhelmed with the image of his smaller truck crashing into the back of the larger white vehicle. When these intrusive memories entered his mind, it was like he experienced the event all over again. This often led to Adam needing to pull over because of how distressing the memories and flashbacks were. Some days, Adam even decided to stay home from work to avoid driving.

Second, we may try to avoid anything that reminds us of the event. This avoidance may involve the inner world, such as trying to avoid thoughts, feelings, memories, or images of the event. Or we may try to avoid the outer world, like the people, places, and experiences that remind us of the original traumatic event. As an example, Hazel grew up in an apartment complex on a busy street in a downtown area. In her childhood years, her mother often physically abused her by hitting her and kicking her for not doing her chores on time or struggling with her homework. Frequently, Hazel was physically wounded from the abuse to the point that she couldn't go to school. Over a decade later, Hazel lived in the same town, yet would avoid driving down the road that her childhood apartment complex was on to avoid the reminder of the physical abuse.

Third, we may experience changes in our thoughts, feelings, and behaviors, such as trouble remembering details about the traumatic event. We may also struggle with negative thoughts about ourselves (e.g., "I'm a horrible person for letting this happen," "It's 100% my fault"), other people (e.g., "Other people are dangerous and out to get me," "People are evil"), or the world around us (e.g., "The world is unsafe," "The world is chaotic and uncertain"). As another example, we may experience distressing emotions like overwhelming sadness, fear, anxiety, guilt, and shame. When this happens, we may struggle to experience any positive emotions (e.g., happiness, joy, contentment) at all. To offer one more example, we may have a hard time being motivated to engage in hobbies or other activities we used to enjoy. For instance, Alex joined a local police department in his early 20s. Quickly, he started to witness extreme violence on the job, such as domestic violence when he would have to respond to 9-1-1 calls coming from houses, and drunk driving accidents that left drivers and passengers severely wounded or dead on the road. Gradually, he started to feel extremely anxious when he would get such calls over the radio. He also ended up thinking negative thoughts about others and the world, such as "The world is a horrible place. No one is safe. Everyone is out for themselves."

Fourth, we may become extremely reactive and irritable after the traumatic event. This may include feeling on edge, nervous, or hypervigilant. We may constantly look over our shoulder or be easily startled. As a quick example, Mariah worked at a gas station as a cashier during the late-night shift. One night, she was robbed at gunpoint by a masked man who yelled at her and demanded all the money in the cash register. After the event, she was easily startled by loud voices and quick movements. She found herself constantly looking over her shoulder to see if someone was behind her with a gun.

When these symptoms—across the above four major categories—are experienced for more than a month and lead to the struggle to carry out daily functioning in work life, family life, or other areas of life, we may be diagnosed with PTSD. For example, Christopher served in the military for several years after the 9/11 terrorist attacks. During his deployment, he witnessed several people being killed. Upon returning home, he got a job at a local bank as a bank teller and was eager to settle back into civilian life. Most days, however, he struggled to do his job well. He was distracted by intrusive memories of people dying in front of him. He also sometimes had a hard time driving to work, given the violence he witnessed while serving in the military often took place when he was driving on patrol. While working at the bank, Christopher also thought to himself that people are "violent by nature." This led to constantly feeling on edge that someone would try to rob the bank on his shift. As a result, he was hypervigilant, which prevented him from being friendly and easygoing with the bank customers he interacted with. Eventually, Christopher could not perform on the job and was terminated because of both customer and coworker complaints.

One theory suggests that these types of traumatic events are so difficult to endure because they destroy our assumptions and core beliefs about the world,[8] or our worldview. All humans have a worldview, which reveals beliefs about God (e.g., whether there's a personal God or no God at all), reality (e.g., whether there is a spiritual reality or just a material world), knowledge (e.g., whether knowledge comes from science or a sacred text like the Bible), values (e.g., morality, virtues), humanity (e.g., whether humans are created in God's image, whether humans are inherently good or bad), and purpose (e.g., whether humans have an ultimate purpose for this life).[9] These worldview ingredients can come from a range of sources and combinations of such sources, like culture and religion. When we experience a traumatic event, our worldview assumptions may "shatter."[10] These augmented beliefs may include whether life is predictable, controllable, and safe and whether other people are safe and trustworthy. When our worldview is disrupted by traumatic events, this can be extremely destabilizing, given our view of the world helps us move through life with confidence and consistency. This change in how we view others and the world (for example, moving from seeing other people and the world as safe, predictable, and controllable to unsafe, unpredictable, and uncontrollable) can give rise to a range of trauma symptoms, such as overwhelming fear, anxiety, and hypervigilance. When this happens, we may struggle to move through daily life in a self-assured manner.

As these symptoms and examples reveal, traumatic events can lead to trauma symptoms that impair daily life, warranting a formal PTSD diagnosis. Of course, not all traumatic events result in a formal PTSD diagnosis. Rather, rates of PTSD can vary. In one recent article that reviewed the occurrence of PTSD in the U.S., findings revealed that the prevalence of PTSD over the life-span can range wildly from about 3% to 27%.[11] These types of findings suggest that most trauma survivors will *not* develop enough symptoms over time and struggle with impaired daily functioning to meet full criteria for a PTSD diagnosis.

Avoidance and Rumination

Still, many trauma survivors will go on to struggle with at least *some* psychological symptoms that get in the way of daily life. Two symptoms that I'd like us to discuss next are avoidance and rumination (with rumination already introduced in Chapter 1). These symptoms are sometimes experienced together and may increase the very symptoms we are trying to get rid of.

Regarding avoidance, we may struggle with difficult inner experiences, such as distressing thoughts, feelings, sensations, memories, and images. When this happens, we may be tempted to try to avoid them as a go-to solution. In secular clinical psychology, this is more formally called "experiential avoidance," or EA. It is defined as "an unwillingness to remain in contact with distressing thoughts, feelings, memories, and other private experiences—even when doing so creates harm in the long run."[12] We may use either cognitive (with our mind) or behavioral (with our actions) avoidance strategies.[13] We may try to distract ourselves from psychological suffering, such as when we think about something else. We may also try to deny our psychological suffering, such as when we suppress what we are feeling. As another example, we may try to avoid psychological suffering at all costs, such as when we use drugs or alcohol to numb the pain. For instance, James grew up in a single-parent home. Then, one day, his mother never came home. From there, James was placed in the foster care system. As an adult, he felt extremely abandoned and alone. He had vivid memories of waiting for his mom to come home, only to have to go to a neighbor's house to ask for help because she never returned from work. To numb himself from these feelings, James began to drink alcohol after work and on the weekends, to the point that he would black out and wake up most days with a hangover.

The problem with EA, for both James and the rest of us, is that it may make our suffering worse. For example, research has found that EA is positively linked to symptoms of depression, phobias, and obsessive-compulsive disorder.[14] This means that when people report more efforts to avoid unpleasant thoughts, feelings, sensations, memories, and images, they report more psychological symptoms.

In the context of traumatic events and trauma symptoms, one study among university students found that EA helped to explain the relationship between students' reported childhood traumatic events (e.g., physical, sexual, or emotional abuse) and current trauma-related symptoms (i.e., PTSD symptoms like intrusive memories, avoidance, negative thoughts and feelings, and hypervigilance).[15] This finding suggests that our current efforts to avoid difficult inner experiences that come from childhood traumatic experiences may actually increase, not decrease, trauma-related symptoms.

Interestingly, one type of avoidance that we may utilize to try to distance ourselves from psychological symptoms is rumination. Although we may not view rumination as a form of avoidance because we intentionally dwell on distressing events and symptoms, many secular psychologists suggest it is an avoidance strategy.[16] Succinctly defined as "obsessional thinking involving excessive, repetitive thoughts or themes,"[17] secular psychologists have historically theorized about and researched rumination in the context of many types of psychological symptoms (e.g., depression, anxiety, trauma).[18] From this perspective, rumination involves focusing our attention on the "causes and consequences" of our symptoms.[19] We may also *think about* our emotions, not actually *feel* them.[20] Rumination may be a form of avoidance, specifically cognitive avoidance, in that we are thinking about the causes and consequences of our symptoms and our symptoms themselves in an overly abstract manner, rather than actually feeling difficult feelings and accepting difficult memories and images.[21] Ruminative thinking is a problem because we need to feel what there is to feel, not think our way out of our feelings,[22] to maintain mental health. In other words, to adequately process difficult experiences, we need to feel the full spectrum of emotions that accompany adversity.

This has led some secular psychologists to contrast two different types of processing in response to psychological suffering—abstract, analytical, ruminative processing and concrete, present-moment, experiential processing.[23] With the former, we may tend to overly focus on verbally processing our emotional pain by asking abstract "Why" questions (e.g., "Why does this always happen to me?"). With the latter, we may commonly focus on feeling our feelings by asking "How" questions (e.g., "How did I feel when it happened?" "How do I feel now?"). With rumination (as a form of abstract processing), our "Why" questions may be unanswerable and leave us stuck on an overly analytical level. When stuck there, we may not be able to process our emotions at a more concrete level, which is needed for psychological health and making sense of our daily experiences.

In the context of trauma, rumination may involve asking such abstract "Why" (e.g., "Why did this happen to me?") and "What if" (e.g., "What if it happens again?") questions.[24] We may ruminate to create some distance from the vivid memory, flashback, or dream and corresponding emotional distress, whether sadness, fear, anxiety, guilt, or shame.[25] In other words, we may use abstract, analytical thinking so we don't have to psychologically and concretely experience the intensity of the event itself in the form of memories and emotions. By asking more abstract "Why" and "What if" questions about the causes and consequence of the traumatic event, we don't have to process the actual emotional impact of the event. Although this makes sense because the emotional pain is so difficult, abstract, analytical "Why" questions can leave us "spinning our wheels," so to speak. We may not be able to drive out of the proverbial mud because we are stuck in a rut.

Although rumination seems to create some necessary distance from our emotional pain, it doesn't work long-term. This is because rumination may paradoxically increase the distressing memories and emotions that we are trying to distance ourselves from.[26] Also, our daily functioning may become impaired because we are distracted from life. To offer a quick example, Melinda was physically abused by a high school boyfriend, which resulted in a sprained wrist and urgent care visit. Although she broke up with him immediately after receiving medical care, she still frequently asked "Why" and "What if" questions when she had flashbacks of him pushing her down. She also felt afraid it would happen again. Over time, she noticed that she would be "lost in her head," analyzing the possible causes of the abuse (e.g., "Why did I let him into my life?" "Why didn't I see the warning signs sooner?") and consequences of it (e.g., "What if I never feel safe to date again?"). Although she wanted to avoid the fear she commonly felt, the rumination seemed to make things worse. She ended up continuing to experience the flashbacks and fear, along with the rumination.

In support of this understanding that ruminative avoidance doesn't work long-term, research has revealed that EA explains the relationship between rumination and PTSD symptoms.[27] In other words, as individuals report more rumination (such as dwelling on what they may have done to change the traumatic event or whether the event will happen to them again), they report more efforts to avoid unpleasant thoughts, feelings, sensations, memories, and images. And the more they report efforts to avoid, the more PTSD symptoms they report. This study suggests that rumination can be a go-to cognitive avoidance strategy, albeit an ineffective one.

In another study, researchers examined whether rumination explains the link between the ability to regulate emotions and symptoms of PTSD.[28] Findings revealed that as participants reported they were less likely to be able to manage their emotions well, they reported more rumination (like repeatedly thinking about why the traumatic event happened or what steps they could have taken to prevent it from happening). Also, as participants reported more rumination, they reported more PTSD symptoms. These results suggest that rumination may be employed as an unhelpful strategy to manage overwhelming emotions in the context of traumatic events and PTSD symptoms.

To offer one more study, researchers investigated the relationship between the number of different types of traumatic events (e.g., witnessing a violent act being inflicted on someone else, being the victim of a violent act), rumination (e.g., thinking about why one feels the way they do), and PTSD symptoms.[29] Findings revealed that rumination explained the link between the number of traumatic events and PTSD symptoms. This means that the more people reported experiencing different types of traumatic events, the more they reported ruminating. Also, the more they reported ruminating, the more PTSD symptoms they stated they suffered from. As another interesting finding in the same study, rumination explained the negative relationship between mindfulness and PTSD symptoms. This means that the more people endorsed the mindful skills of awareness and acceptance of difficult inner experiences, the less they reported ruminating and, in turn, PTSD symptoms.

Overall, these studies suggest that when we experience a traumatic event, we may use abstract thinking—ruminating on "Why" and "What if" questions related to the causes and consequences of traumatic events and thinking about, not feeling, difficult trauma-based emotions—to avoid experiencing the distressing trauma-related memories and emotions.[30] For instance, when we experience the death of someone we love, instead of facing and processing the corresponding memories and emotions (which is certainly difficult to do and takes time), we may ruminate with more analytical "Why" questions to avoid having to experience the emotional pain, accept the reality of the loss, and grieve the loss.[31] In other words, rumination is an ineffective emotion regulation strategy that doesn't work.[32]

I can personally attest to this. I notice that when I inevitably get stuck in cycles of rumination, I am not allowing myself to feel my emotions. Instead, I am pursuing more analytical, abstract answers to "Why" questions. I become a philosopher that overly thinks when I need to be an artist who feels. As a result, I've learned to notice the rumination from a place of non-judgment (saying to myself something like "Although this doesn't work, it's simply my attempt to protect myself from emotional pain"), then gently shift toward feeling what there is to feel (saying to myself something like "It's understandable I feel sad right now"). In other words, I've learned to shift from abstract to concrete processing.

Unfortunately, when we turn to rumination, which we are all prone to doing, we may not successfully process our memories and emotions. Instead, our PTSD symptoms may increase, despite our best efforts to eradicate them. Therefore, researchers have attempted to develop interventions to help trauma survivors better process traumatic events and their resulting trauma symptoms.

Trauma Interventions

Within CBT, a popular and well-researched type of psychotherapy first mentioned in Chapter 1, there are many interventions for trauma symptoms. Research has revealed that, in general, these CBT interventions can be helpful in reducing trauma symptoms among trauma survivors.[33] For example, prolonged exposure (PE) treatment helps trauma survivors to experience, not avoid, their trauma-related memories and corresponding emotional reactions (e.g., anxiety, fear).[34] They may be asked to imagine the traumatic event via memories and images in the psychotherapy office or face reminders of the traumatic event out in the real world. Over time, the idea is that trauma survivors will learn to experience trauma-related memories without such intense emotional reactions (which can lead to problematic forms of avoidance and impaired daily living). By facing, not avoiding via rumination, the memory and emotion, survivors are able to recognize such memories and emotions are just inner experiences, not events happening in the real world. They may also gain new insights into the event and recognize that they can handle difficult symptoms when they arise. In turn, they may gain confidence in their ability to navigate life again. To date, research on various types of PE-based therapies has revealed it is helpful in reducing trauma symptoms among trauma survivors.[35]

One of the newer interventions for PTSD is mindfulness-based therapy (briefly introduced in Chapter 1). This type of therapy is also housed within the CBT literature, beyond more traditional approaches for trauma like PE-related therapies. Because mindfulness-based practices help practitioners to focus on the present moment (not the past or future) by connecting directly to sensory experiences (rather than judging and ruminating with an overly evaluative, critical mind),[36] they may be helpful for trauma symptoms and trauma-based rumination.

More formally, mindfulness can be defined as "the capacity to maintain awareness of, and openness to, immediate experience—including internal mental states, thoughts, feelings, memories, and impinging elements of the external world—without judgment and with acceptance."[37] Mindfulness can be used informally as a set of skills for relating to the inner world (whether thoughts, feelings, sensations, memories, or images) or outer world (whether interpersonal exchanges or activities). It can also be used as a formal meditative practice when we set aside designated time to practice, for example, mindful walking or mindful breathing. One reason mindfulness (again, either as a set of skills applied to all of life or as a meditative practice) may be helpful for trauma is that it allows trauma survivors to relate differently to trauma-based symptoms—via non-judgmental awareness and acceptance of whatever is happening in the present moment—rather than resorting to avoidance. In that ruminative avoidance doesn't work in the long-run, mindfulness-based approaches offer a helpful alternative.

In support of this understanding, a study revealed that, among a sample of adults who recently experienced a traumatic event, mindfulness (as a set of skills, not formal practice) was negatively associated with thought suppression (that is, attempting to suppress distressing thoughts), which was positively associated with rumination.[38] This finding suggests that those who endorsed more mindful skills in daily life (e.g., present-moment awareness, non-judgmental awareness, and acceptance of difficult inner experiences) reported they were less likely to try to suppress difficult thoughts and, in turn, less likely to ruminate. In terms of research on actual mindfulness-based interventions/practices, a review article found that mindfulness-based interventions were helpful in reducing symptoms of PTSD.[39]

Specific mindfulness-based interventions for PTSD and other trauma symptoms may include mindfulness of breathing (wherein we focus on the breath in the present moment, then non-judgmentally bring our attention back to the breath when we begin to ruminate in response to trauma-based memories and emotions).[40] Or we may engage in mindfully noticing our environment in the present moment with our senses (using our sense of sight, for example, to non-judgmentally notice several things in the room we are in, then non-judgmentally bringing our attention back to our sense of sight when we begin to ruminate in response to trauma-based memories and emotions).[41] Really, we can apply the core mindful skills—attention, focus on the present moment, awareness, and acceptance[42]—to all kinds of informal (e.g., mindfully brushing our teeth, mindfully walking the dog) and formal (e.g., mindfully noticing our emotions, mindfully noticing our thoughts, mindfully breathing, mindfully walking) activities.

With these types of practices applied to trauma symptoms, we are learning to notice trauma-related memories, emotions, and rumination, then apply a non-judgmental, open, curious attitude toward them in the present moment. Instead of ruminating as a form of cognitive avoidance, we are learning to be with our symptoms. By accepting them with non-judgment, which is by no means an easy task, we are not only learning to be with them and make room for them, which is a more effective strategy than avoidance, we are also improving our life. This is because we are letting go of rumination and avoidance as our go-to strategy. We are no longer stuck ruminating about why things turned out the way they did and why they should have been different. We are recognizing that, pragmatically, rumination doesn't work, even though it is tempting. Before concluding the chapter, I'd like to introduce two brief exercises, then end with a case example to bring a secular psychological understanding of trauma into the real world.

Exercises

Trauma Symptom Checklist

For the first of two exercises in this chapter, I'd like for you to spend the next day monitoring your symptoms of trauma (see Table 2.1). Please document the trauma-related symptoms you are experiencing at least three times for the day. If you need a review of the main categories of symptoms, feel free to return to the previous discussion on trauma symptoms from this chapter. Upon recording your symptoms, you will be gaining a greater awareness of them as we head into the four skill-based chapters. This preliminary practice will help you begin to relate differently to your symptoms—first, by simply noticing you have them—as we invite God to be with us in subsequent chapters. Please use extra paper if needed.

Let's now turn to one more exercise, then a case example to conclude the chapter.

Non-Judgmental Noticing

For the last exercise in the chapter,[43] I'd like for us to build on the previous exercise by non-judgmentally acknowledging the trauma-based symptoms we are experiencing in the inner world right here and now. Then, I'd like us to practice non-judgmentally noticing our environment in the outer world, also right here and now. Eventually, in subsequent chapters, we will be more deliberately applying this strategy—non-judgmental awareness and acceptance of the present moment—to the inner world (including trauma-based memories, emotions, and rumination) as we practice God's presence and invite God to be with us in our pain in the immediacy of each moment. Yet, for now, we are simply beginning the process of relating to inner and outer experiences with non-judgmental, present-moment awareness and acceptance.

To begin, find a quiet environment, free from distractions. Sit up straight in a supportive chair. When you are ready, start by turning to your inner world. This will be followed by noticing your outer world.

TABLE 2.1
Trauma Symptom Checklist

	Type of Intrusive Memories/ Images/Dreams/ Flashbacks	Type of Avoidance of Inner Experiences (Thoughts, Feelings, Sensations, Memories, or Images) or Outer Experiences (People, Places, Things, Other)	Type of Distressing Thoughts (About the Self, Others, or the World) or Emotions (Fear, Anxiety, Sadness, Anger, Guilt, Shame, Helplessness, Other)	Type of Reactivity (Easily Startled, On Edge, Hypervigilant, Other)	Type of Rumination ("Why" Questions, "What If" Questions, Dwelling on Emotions, Dwelling on Causes or Consequences of Event, Other)
Morning					
Mid-Day					
Evening					

1. Simply become aware of, from a place of non-judgment, what is going on inside. Try to become aware of what you might be experiencing with your thoughts, feelings, sensations, memories, and images, whether pleasant or unpleasant or wanted or unwanted. As you do so, try to apply an attitude of non-judgment. This means that you are refraining from evaluating or criticizing your psychological experience as right or wrong or good or bad. Instead, you are open to whatever comes up. You are just noticing, from a place of awareness and acceptance, what is emerging in the inner world in the immediacy of this moment.

2. Use your sense of sight to notice five things in the room you are in, also from a place of non-judgment. Refrain from evaluating the experience as not quite right in some way. Rather, just allow the experience to unfold with an open curiosity. You may notice the texture of the carpet under your feet or the design of the clock on the wall. You may notice the color of the walls around you or the shapes and contours of a piece of furniture. As you notice, try to also apply an attitude of non-judgment to what you are experiencing, this time directed toward the outer world in the immediacy of this moment.

We'll revisit this strategy in subsequent chapters, doing so from a distinctly Christian perspective. In the meantime, I'd like to share a case to help you better understand the relationship between traumatic events, trauma symptoms, and mindfulness-based interventions.

Case Example

Gregory grew up in a middle-class neighborhood with loving parents and a supportive network of friends and family. After high school, he started delivering pizzas to make enough money for a monthly car payment. During most evenings, he would deliver pizzas. He filled his days attending community college, studying, and doing homework.

With a job, school, and friends and family to spend time with, Gregory's life was full. He was relatively happy and making progress toward his dream of attending an out-of-state college to study to be an engineer. Yet, on one weeknight, he was delivering a pizza to an apartment complex that wasn't well lit. Upon getting out of his car, he noticed two young adults with hoods over their heads lurking in the distance. As he walked by them, they summoned him to come talk to them. Although Gregory needed to get back to the pizza parlor, he decided to talk to them to see what they wanted.

As he approached them, one of the men pointed a gun at Gregory and demanded all his money. Carrying about $100 in cash from prior deliveries, Gregory quickly gave up what he had, looking down at the ground out of fear. For a moment, Gregory didn't know if he would be shot, beaten up, or simply robbed. After a few seconds, the two men grabbed the money, then took his car keys and drove off with his car.

Stranded in a relatively unfamiliar part of town and without a phone or money to make a call, Gregory had to walk several miles to get back to the pizza parlor. There, he told his manager what happened, spoke with the police to file a report, and went home in a state of shock.

That night, he woke up from a nightmare that involved the two men shooting him to finish the job. In the middle of the night in his bed, he was terrified. He felt an overwhelming sense of fear and uncertainty, wondering if they would find out where he lived and come to take his life. For several weeks, Gregory was on edge, easily startled, and fearful that he would see the two men again. Any sound at night was interpreted as the men coming to get him. He also increasingly asked a variety of questions that seemed to offer no real answers: "Why did they rob me?" "Why was I targeted?" "What if I'm robbed again?" "What if I'm killed?"

Following about two months of emotional suffering, he decided to go to a therapist to get help. On a Tuesday morning about ten weeks after the traumatic event, he greeted Dr. Clemens in a small office close to his home. There, she began to talk with him about the symptoms of PTSD. Among other symptoms, they discussed Gregory's struggle with nightmares and flashbacks of the gun being pointed in his face. They also explored Gregory's overwhelming fear and uncertainty, as well as his recurrent thought that the world was no longer a safe place. Dr. Clemens also educated Gregory about the common experience of trauma-based rumination, which he could identify with.

After a few sessions to get to know one another and assess Gregory's current functioning, Dr. Clemens diagnosed Gregory with PTSD. From there, they began to develop a treatment plan, which included, among other strategies, mindfulness meditation. In the office, Dr. Clemens worked with Gregory to notice, with non-judgmental awareness and acceptance, when he was struggling with rumination. Instead of continuing to ruminate, she asked him to simply maintain an awareness of his rumination without judging it or evaluating it. She also asked him to notice other trauma symptoms he was experiencing, such as the flashbacks and corresponding fear. Gradually, Gregory was able to notice these symptoms, then shift toward a more mindful awareness of his environment to anchor himself to the here-and-now. Rather than continuing to ruminate with unanswerable "Why" and "What if" questions in response to the flashbacks and fear, he could notice when he was stuck, then gently shift toward an awareness of his environment.

Although Gregory would work with Dr. Clemens for several more months to process the traumatic event more fully with PE therapy, this initial strategy of noticing his trauma symptoms, then gently pivoting to his environment in the immediacy of the moment, helped him to begin to relate differently to his inner world.

Conclusion

To conclude this chapter, most individuals will end up suffering from one or more traumatic events in our lifetime. These events may take place in childhood, as ACEs, or later in life. These traumatic events can be extremely destabilizing, leading to changed worldview assumptions as we move from seeing the world and other people as safe, predictable, and controllable to unsafe, unpredictable, and uncontrollable. A smaller portion of individuals will go on to struggle with a range of more enduring trauma symptoms, some of whom will be diagnosed with PTSD. Even without a formal diagnosis, intrusive memories and distressing emotions may get in the way of daily living. In response, some of us may struggle with rumination as an ineffective cognitive avoidance strategy. We may begin to ruminate, asking unanswerable "Why" and "What if" questions about the causes and consequences of traumatic events. We may employ ruminative thinking as an overly abstract way to distance ourselves from our most difficult trauma-related memories and emotions. Yet, this strategy may not work, long-term, since we are not able to fully process the emotional experience and, instead, may make our trauma symptoms worse.

Mindfulness-based interventions may be helpful in allowing us to relate differently to trauma symptoms, moving from avoidance and rumination to non-judgmental, present-moment awareness and acceptance. Yet, for Christian trauma survivors, we may not want to simply accept difficult symptoms for pragmatic reasons—because avoidance and rumination don't work. Also, mindfulness originates from the Buddhist religious tradition. Although there is some debate about whether the version of mindfulness that is embedded in CBT has been sufficiently stripped of its Buddhist roots, many Christian trauma survivors may wish to turn to our own Christian heritage for meditative strategies.[44] In other words, as Christians, we may wish to better understand traumatic events from within the context of a Christian worldview, which we'll be covering in the next chapter. From there, I'll be presenting a four-skill approach for Christian trauma survivors that draws upon the best of secular psychological science but with a solid Christian foundation. This integrative approach—a four-skill, Christian-based strategy for shifting from trauma-based rumination to God—has been confirmed in my own original research[45] to be helpful for Christian trauma survivors such as yourself.

Notes

1. Benjet et al. (2016).
2. Benjet et al. (2016, p. 2).
3. Felitti et al. (1998, p. 246).
4. Felitti et al. (1998, p. 246).
5. "Parental separation or divorce" was later added to the ACEs categories (Dube et al., 2001).
6. Frewen et al. (2019).
7. APA (2022).
8. Schuler and Boals (2016).
9. Knabb et al. (2025).
10. Schuler and Boals (2016).
11. Schein et al. (2021).
12. Gámez et al. (2011).
13. This summary of the different types of EA is based on Gámez et al. (2011).
14. Gámez et al. (2011).
15. Lewis and Naugle (2017).
16. See, for example, Dickson et al. (2012).
17. APA Dictionary (n.d.e).
18. See, for example, Dickson et al. (2012).
19. Nolen-Hoeksema et al. (1993).
20. Teasdale et al. (2014).
21. Dickson et al. (2012).
22. Crane (2009).
23. Leigh et al. (2025); Santa Maria et al. (2012); Watkins (2008).
24. Michael et al. (2007).
25. Ehlers and Clark (2000).
26. Michael et al. (2007).
27. Bishop et al. (2018).
28. Ehring and Ehlers (2014).
29. Im and Follette (2016).
30. Walser and Hayes (2006).
31. Stroebe et al. (2007).
32. Miethe et al. (2023).
33. Lewis et al. (2020).
34. This review of PE is based on Nacasch et al. (2015).
35. McLean et al. (2022).
36. Follette et al. (2006).
37. Briere (2015, p. 14).
38. Nitzan-Assayag et al. (2015).
39. Hopwood and Schutte (2017).
40. Follette and Pistorello (2007).
41. Follette and Pistorello (2007).
42. Feldman et al. (2007).
43. This exercise is based on a review of Harris' (2019) "Dropping Anchor" exercise.
44. See, e.g., Knabb and Vazquez (2025).
45. Knabb et al. (2019a, 2019c); Knabb et al. (2022).

CHAPTER 3

Trauma

A Christian Perspective

Introduction

Within the third chapter of this workbook, we'll explore a Christian understanding of suffering. This includes traumatic events and trauma symptoms in a fallen, broken world. We'll discuss scriptural support and classic spiritual writings from the three branches of Christianity to unpack a Christian view of suffering. Examples of the Christian sources we'll review include 16th and 17th century Protestant writings on God's promises, 17th century Catholic writings on practicing the presence of God, 4th to 15th century Orthodox writings on calling on the name of Jesus, and 16th century Catholic writings on "finding God in all things." Overall, we'll emphasize a distinctly Christian understanding of the problem of and solution to trauma-based suffering in preparation for the subsequent skill-based chapters. To end, I offer two exercises, then provide a real-life story of a Christian trauma survivor to strengthen and encourage you.

Suffering from a Christian Perspective

To start this chapter, I'd like us to explore a Christian view of suffering. We'll consider the grand narrative of the Bible that spans Genesis to Revelation. This

DOI: 10.4324/9781003647270-3

meta-story elucidates a Christian worldview, or comprehensive view of God, reality, knowledge acquisition, values, humanity, and humanity's purpose in this world. Unfortunately, when Christians experience traumatic events, our once-solid Christian worldview may be questioned, become tenuous, or even "shatter."[1] This shattered view of the world may lead to added uncertainty after a traumatic event. We may not only have to struggle with intrusive memories of the traumatic event and corresponding distressing emotions but also doubts about who God is, his presence or absence amid trauma-related suffering, and his plan and ultimate purpose for us in our trauma-related suffering.

The Grand Narrative of Scripture

According to Genesis, the first book of the Bible, God created Adam and Eve. They were to take care of the Garden of Eden. In the Garden, they were naked and felt no shame as newly formed humans. During this time, they were in right relationship with God. As their one prohibition, God commanded them not to eat from the tree of the knowledge of good and evil. Yet, as the famous story goes, they consumed fruit from the forbidden tree. Once this happened, according to Genesis 3, they realized they were naked and covered themselves to hide. As the penalty for disobeying God and rebelling against his command, suffering entered the world. Because of the fall, we now have physical, psychological, relational, and spiritual suffering. God clothed Adam and Eve and banished them from the safety and comfort of both the Garden and being in right relationship with him. Here, in Genesis 2 and 3, we have both the human account of creation and the fall of Adam and Eve and, subsequently, the rest of humankind.

Fast-forward to the gospels within the New Testament of the Bible, and we read about God sending his Son, Jesus Christ, to die for humankind so that we can be reconciled to God and have eternal life with God.[2] Specifically, God became a human being, Jesus Christ, so he could die on a cross.[3] By dying on a cross and being raised from the dead, Christians believe that Jesus paid the penalty of death for our sins so that we can have eternal life with God and one day be raised from the dead, too.[4] In fact, when we "declare with [our] mouth, 'Jesus is Lord,' and believe in [our] heart that God raised him from the dead, [we] will be saved."[5] This plan of redemption offered by God allows Christians to be reconciled to, not estranged from, him.[6] At the very end of the New Testament, in the book of Revelation, we read about God's plan of restoration. Christians will be with God in heaven, where there will be no more suffering, and God will create a new heaven and earth.[7]

As Christians, we, too, are part of this grand story of the Bible. This includes our own struggles with suffering in a fallen, broken world. Yet, since

God took on human form as Jesus Christ, he understands our weaknesses and struggles.[8] Jesus is available for us to come to him when we need his mercy, or loving-kindness, and grace, or undeserved merit or favor.[9] This overarching account from the Bible—with the four main stages of creation, fall, redemption, and restoration—can help us to understand who God is, his plan for us, and how we are to make sense of suffering, including traumatic events and trauma symptoms.

A Christian Worldview

For Christians, the Bible is God's Word, or divine revelation. This means that God chose to reveal himself to us via the Bible. He didn't just reveal who he is through his creation, called general revelation. Although he certainly reveals who he is in his design of the world (for example, his infinite power by creating vast mountain landscapes and oceans), he also chose to reveal himself personally via Scripture. Spanning several thousand years, the Bible tells the story of God's creation of the world, his pursuit of humankind, even when we turn away from and rebel against him, and his plan for us. Even though we continue to sin in a fallen world, God chose to die for us.[10] This act of love has far-reaching implications for Christians, given God offers us a plan to save us. Based on God's plan, we have hope that our current suffering is by no means permanent. Rather, our suffering is temporary, and God will eventually eradicate all suffering.

In this story from Genesis to Revelation, we learn about the main ingredients of a cohesive and coherent Christian worldview.[11] First, we learn about who God is and God's providence. God is infinitely loving,[12] wise,[13] powerful,[14] and present.[15] We learn that God's providence—or his active, purposeful, good governance and protective care—extends to all of creation, including humankind.[16] This means that we have a benevolent, powerful King watching over his kingdom. God's unique combination of infinite love/goodness, wisdom, power, and presence means he wants what is best for us, knows all possible scenarios, has the power to carry out the best scenario, and is present through it all. In the context of trauma-related suffering, this means that God has not withdrawn himself from the cares of the world. Instead, he works things out for good,[17] even when we do not fully understand his purposes and will. We'll unpack this important understanding in subsequent chapters.

Second, we learn about a view of reality, namely that there is a physical world that God created, along with a spiritual, transcendent reality. Throughout Scripture, we read about this spiritual reality, beyond what we can experience with the five senses in the physical world.[18] When considering trauma-related suffering, although we currently live in a fallen, broken, imperfect world, God is with us. We will one day be face-to-face with God in heaven. In heaven, there will be no more trauma-related suffering.[19] We'll explore this salient theme in forthcoming chapters.

Third, we learn that the Bible is trustworthy as a source of knowledge and guide for life. In the Old Testament, we read that the Bible can help us in our daily experiences.[20] In the New Testament, we read that "all Scripture is God-breathed and is useful for teaching, rebuking, correcting and training in righteousness..."[21] In relation to trauma-related suffering, we can turn to God's Word, the Bible, to offer trustworthy guidance for daily life, especially when traumatic events cause confusion, instability, and doubt. Across the four skill-based chapters, we'll draw upon Scripture to relate differently to trauma-related suffering.

Fourth, we learn about a wide variety of virtues, or moral behaviors, for daily living. These virtues range from the Ten Commandments,[22] to Jesus' Sermon on the Mount,[23] to the Apostle Paul's teachings on both the fruit of the Spirit[24] and our need to focus on "things above" not "earthly things."[25] Indeed, the entire four-skill program in this workbook was inspired by Paul's instructions to shift from earthly- to heavenly-mindedness when we struggle with trauma-related rumination. Thus, Scripture offers a range of key tools to help us in our time of need.

Fifth, we learn about who we are as human beings. We are sinful (yet still loved by God) and in need of God's grace to be restored to a right relationship with him. This means that no matter what we've experienced in a fallen, broken world, nothing can keep us from God's love: "Who shall separate us from the love of Christ? Shall trouble or hardship or persecution or famine or nakedness or danger or sword?"[26] When considering trauma-related suffering, this scriptural truth means that we can practice God's presence during our trauma-related struggles, such as when we feel overwhelmed by intrusive memories and distressing emotions.

Finally, we learn about our purpose in this world—"to glorify God, and enjoy him forever."[27] Even though trauma-related suffering can be disorienting and chip away at our Christian worldview, as Christian trauma survivors, we can hold on to our ultimate purpose. This purpose is to be in right relationship with God. We are to commune/fellowship with God as we trek through this difficult life.[28] These ingredients of a Christian worldview—views about God, reality, knowledge acquisition, values, humanity, and purpose—help us to make sense of our fallen, broken, and sometimes dangerous, world.

In my own original research, I've developed with colleagues a Christian Worldview Scale, which measures Christian beliefs about God, knowledge acquisition, values, humanity, and ultimate meaning/purpose.[29] In this published study, we gave the Christian Worldview Scale to Christians in the community alongside several other measures that assess psychological functioning. We found that a Christian worldview was positively related to well-being and negatively related to symptoms of depression, anxiety, and stress. This means that as Christians reported living out a Christian worldview, they reported greater well-being (e.g., relaxation, optimism) and fewer symptoms of depression (e.g., low mood), anxiety (e.g., worry), and stress (e.g., overreactivity, agitation). From this study, we can see that a Christian worldview has important mental health implications. Therefore, throughout this workbook, I will be turning to a Christian worldview to make sense of trauma-related suffering.

To offer another original study, I researched with several colleagues the idea that trusting in and surrendering to God's providence can be helpful for accepting the uncertainties of life and, consequently, reducing worry among Christian chronic worriers.[30] Findings revealed that as Christians endorsed positive beliefs about God's providence, they also reported a greater willingness to surrender to God as a form of coping during times of adversity. And as they reported a greater willingness to surrender to God, they reported a greater willingness to accept the uncertainties of life and, consequently, less worry. This study suggests that Christians can benefit, mental-health-wise, from deepening our trust in God's providence so we can yield to his will and let go of chronic, repetitious worry. This is especially powerful if worry is about trying to attain certainty in an uncertain, ambiguous world, which will never fully happen on this side of heaven. In other words, worry is about trying to predict the future and gain a sense of control over an unknown future, something we can't do as finite humans with a limited mind. In the context of trauma-related suffering, we can learn to trust in God's active, loving presence when we get overwhelmed by trauma-related intrusive memories and emotions, rather than resorting to ruminative thinking. We can shift our focus from unhealthy rumination to ruminating (in a healthy way) on God's Word, the Bible.

Although these studies lend support to the idea that a Christian worldview can be helpful for Christian mental health, traumatic events may damage our Christian worldview by introducing doubt and uncertainty where confidence and certainty used to be present. And this "shattered" worldview has implications for trauma symptoms.[31] We may ask ruminative questions about who God is ("Why would God allow this event to happen if he is supposed to be omnipresent?") and God's providence ("What if God is apathetic, rather than personally caring for me?") in response to the traumatic event. After a traumatic event, we may ruminate on whether God exists (e.g., "What if there is no God?") or whether we can trust the Bible as a guide for life (e.g., "What if the Bible is not divinely inspired?"). As another possibility, we may doubt God's love for us as fallen human beings (e.g., "What if God is punishing me and I'm not saved?") after a traumatic event occurred. Finally, we may question whether there is any sense of morality or ultimate purpose in life (e.g., "What if there is no God, no right and wrong, and no meaning in the world?").

When we suffer from a traumatic event, these types of questions may come flooding in, with no real answers that truly satisfy or help us to feel safe again. Questioning God during seasons of suffering can certainly be a healthy approach to process our pain, given it is biblical. In fact, the lament psalms within the Book of Psalms[32] help us to see that we can cry out to God in sadness, grief, and confusion. We can ask God questions about suffering to process our painful experiences on this side of heaven. We can express our uncertainty, doubt, and ambivalence to him in a direct and authentic manner.

However, we may keep asking unanswerable "Why" questions in a more repetitive and compulsive manner when we get overwhelmed with trauma-related intrusive memories and distressing emotions. Our laments may quickly turn into perseverative rumination, which can make matters worse. This is because the unwanted memories are so vivid, the emotions are so upsetting, and the worldview we previously relied on for a sense of safety, control, predictability, and certainty seems to be in pieces. When we struggle in these excruciating ways, we may just want the pain to go away. Thus, healthy lament may quickly develop into unhealthy rumination as our go-to cognitive avoidance strategy. Let's review this in a bit more detail, before turning to some possible solutions to the dilemma of a shattered Christian worldview.

A Shattered Christian Worldview

Remember from Chapter 2 that traumatic events can sometimes lead to several main types of trauma symptoms. These symptoms include intrusive memories (e.g., vivid images, flashbacks, nightmares), distressing emotions (e.g., fear, anxiety, guilt, shame), attempts to avoid reminders of the event in the inner or outer world, negative views of ourselves, others, and the world, and hypervigilance and an on-edge feeling.[33] Regarding changes to our beliefs, when we experience a traumatic event, this may lead to uncertainty and doubt about others and the world. We may move from the view that others and the world are safe, predictable, and controllable to the perspective that others and the world are unsafe, unpredictable, and uncontrollable. We may even struggle with our beliefs about God. This is why traumatic events can be so destabilizing for Christians.

When a traumatic event occurs, it may be hard to reconcile what has happened with our previously stable, enduring beliefs about the world.[34] We may have a hard time making sense of the gap between how things are and how we thought they were supposed to be. For Christians, not only may we have altered beliefs about ourselves, others, and the world, we may have altered beliefs about God. These altered beliefs about God can chip away at our previous confidence in our Christian worldview. Yet, we need our Christian worldview, both psychologically and spiritually, to make sense of suffering and respond to it.

Several decades ago, the psychologist Ronnie Janoff-Bulman wrote *Shattered Assumptions: Towards a New Psychology of Trauma*.[35] In this important line of work (briefly introduced in Chapter 2), the author suggested that many humans have certain worldview assumptions and core beliefs that we carry with us in life: "The world is benevolent," "The world is meaningful," and "The self is worthy."[36] These assumptions help us to get through life with needed confidence. They allow us to navigate an often uncertain, ambiguous, and imperfect world with self-assurance. Without these assumptions, life would be experienced as overly chaotic and random, which, for many of us, would be too overwhelming and destabilizing. When we experience a traumatic event, it can disrupt our view that the world is a good place, the world has meaning, and people are good.

For Christians, though, we believe that the fall of humankind meant that sin and suffering entered the world. This offers us an explanation for why there are traumatic events and trauma symptoms. God did not originally design the world and humans to experience suffering. Rather, because of free will, humans chose to rebel against God and, consequently, invite sin and suffering into daily life. Because of this, the world is not always good, nor are people. And although Christians believe our existence has meaning, it is not always easy to hold onto because of all the human pain we observe and experience. In other words, like non-Christians, Christians can easily become disoriented and lose sight of the ultimate meaning for life.

Although Christians believe humans are sinful and suffering exists because of the fall, we also believe that God is infinitely good, powerful, wise, and present. This combination of infinite goodness and power (or, taken together, providence) means that he is purposefully guiding his creation toward the best possible plan. As a result, when a traumatic event occurs, we may struggle to comprehend how a benevolent God who works things out for good could allow such an event in our own life. This is especially confusing if we consider that God is a God of love who knows all possible outcomes and has the power and presence to choose what is best. This has been referred to by one Puritan author, John Flavel, as the *Mystery of Providence*.[37] Nonetheless, although Christians do not always know God's mysterious purposes, which can create added confusion, we can choose to trust in his providential care because we trust in *him* as infinitely loving and powerful.

Interestingly, in a U.S. survey that was published several years ago, Christian adults were asked about their views on suffering.[38] First, when asked about "why suffering exists in the world," over 60% of Christians said that "To provide an opportunity for people to come out stronger" either "Very well" or "Somewhat well" explained their perspective. With this same question, over

80% of Christians stated that "Sometimes bad things just happen" either "Very well" or "Somewhat well" explained their perspective. When asked if they get angry at God for "allowing so much suffering in the world," over 80% of Christians answered "Rarely" or "Never." Finally, when asked whether suffering in the world leads to their "doubt that God is all-powerful" or "doubt that God is entirely loving and kind," over 80% of Christians said that either "Not too well" or "Not at all" explained their perspective. These survey results suggest that most U.S. Christian adults do not seem to doubt God's infinite power or love when suffering occurs. Still, for trauma survivors who have directly experienced a traumatic event, such questions may still arise. Throughout Christian history, in fact, Christians have wrestled with the "Why" questions of trauma-related suffering, discussed next.

A Christian Worldview and Suffering

For centuries, Christians have struggled with perspectives on trauma-related suffering in daily life. Why does an infinitely loving, wise, powerful, and present God, who providentially cares for his creation, allow trauma-related suffering? Some possible Christian views on trauma-related suffering may include the following:[39]

- ❏ Sin entered the world due to the fall of humankind, leading to trauma-related suffering.[40]
- ❏ God allows trauma-related suffering so he can suffer with us.[41]
- ❏ God allows trauma-related suffering so we can suffer like Christ.[42]
- ❏ God allows trauma-related suffering so we can help others.[43]
- ❏ God allows trauma-related suffering so we can glorify God and model to others how to effectively respond to suffering.[44]
- ❏ God allows trauma-related suffering to test and refine us.[45]
- ❏ God allows trauma-related suffering so we can hope and put our faith in him.[46]
- ❏ God allows trauma-related suffering so humans can grow psychologically and spiritually.[47]
- ❏ God allows trauma-related suffering so he can providentially work things out for good as part of his larger plan.[48]
- ❏ God allows trauma-related suffering to punish us because he loves us.[49]

Of note, this list is not exhaustive, and I have not prioritized it in order of importance or agreement. Also, some of these reasons may overlap with one another. In either case, one way to organize this list into higher-level categories is to make sense of Christian reasons for trauma-related suffering from "causal" and "functional" views.[50] With causal views, we may ask "Why" questions ("Why did you allow this, God?") to explore why God was somehow involved in the trauma-related suffering.[51] We may prioritize trying to understand and focus on the *source* of trauma-related suffering.[52] Our concern, with this view, pertains to God as the source. With functional views, however, we may ask "What" questions ("What is your plan/will/outcome, God?") and "How" questions ("How are you helping me to grow, God?") to understand God's *purpose* for the trauma-related suffering.[53] Our concern, with this view, relates to God's purpose, not God as the source. For many Christians, we may prioritize dwelling on *either* a causal source *or* functional purpose. As an alternative, we may combine both causal and functional views in pursuit of *both* a source for *and* purpose of our trauma-related suffering. Nevertheless, there seems to be biblical support for a range of Christian views of trauma-related suffering.

We may end up getting stuck in cycles of unhelpful trauma-based rumination when we continue to ask ourselves causal, source questions, such as "Why did you allow this, God?" "Why didn't you prevent this, God?" "Why did an infinitely loving and powerful God allow this to happen?" and "Why are you punishing me, God?" For instance, Sherry had a near-death experience while on a skiing trip with members of her local church. Skiing down a steep slope, she crashed into a tree that she did not see. After losing consciousness and breaking her neck and leg, she was quickly transported to a local hospital. While in the hospital, she had vivid nightmares of crashing into the tree. During these nightmares, she was stranded with no one to rescue her. She would cry out for help, with no one around to hear her screams. Waking up in the hospital after such dreams, she would begin to ruminate on the reasons for the accident. Was God punishing her? Did she have unconfessed sin in her life? Did God withhold his protection for some unknown reason? Dwelling on God as the cause prevented her from having to process the difficult memory. Through rumination, she also attempted to avoid feeling the extreme fear and loneliness she was struggling with while in the hospital.

Rather than dwelling on questions about the source of traumatic events, it may be helpful to move to more functional purpose/plan/outcome questions. More beneficial questions may include "What are you revealing to me in the midst of my trauma-related suffering, God?" and "How are you helping me to draw closer to you after the traumatic event, God?" As an example, Allen had a heart attack while working alone one night at work. With no one else around, he started to feel pain in his chest, and he was unable to breathe. Since no one was around, he experienced extreme fear, with his life flashing before his eyes. Somehow, he was able to call 9-1-1 and get an ambulance to rush to his aid. Weeks later, he was able to cope with this traumatic event by viewing God as with him to help him survive. Instead of asking questions about the cause of the heart attack and focusing on God as the source of his suffering, he thought about the ways in which God was present. He also asked God, in his prayer life, to reveal to him the purpose of the medical emergency so he could grow closer to God, not doubt God's goodness.

With a causal approach, we may never come up with satisfying answers and, instead, continue to ruminate. Causal questions have been debated by philosophers and theologians for ages and ages. This is the problem of theodicy: How can an infinitely good, wise, powerful, and present God allow evil, including trauma-related suffering, in the world? The best and brightest philosophers and theologians of every time period have wrestled with this question, with no universally agreed-upon answer.

On the other hand, with a functional approach, we can emphasize God's presence, what he is doing in and through our trauma-based suffering, and where he is leading us. If a Christian worldview offers us meaning amid trauma-based suffering, whether we prioritize a causal or functional perspective may be key. Although we'll explore this shift from causal, source questions to God's functional presence in greater detail in subsequent chapters, for now, I simply want to highlight that there are a range of biblically derived views of trauma-based suffering. These views may pragmatically lead to better or worse outcomes, psychologically and spiritually.

Pivoting from Rumination to God: An Integrative Understanding

Building on the content we've covered thus far, I'd like to offer an integrative understanding of the need to pivot from unhealthy rumination to God. For Christians, a biblically tethered worldview offers a comprehensive way of understanding reality. This is especially important for suffering, given humans inevitably strive to attain meaning in response to life's adversities.[54] We rely on our views of God, reality, knowledge acquisition, values, humanity, and purpose to get through life. This worldview offers us a sense of consistency, predictability, safety, and control in a fallen, broken world. When we experience a traumatic event, however, we may end up struggling to hold on to this worldview. After such a traumatic event, we may struggle with intrusive memories, like flashbacks, vivid images, and nightmares. These unwanted memories may give rise to an array of distressing emotions, like fear, anxiety, guilt, and shame. When we suffer from difficult trauma-related memories and emotions, we may question our worldview. Because it may feel like we are reliving the traumatic event repeatedly—with vivid flashbacks and overwhelming feelings—we may feel like the world is now unsafe, unpredictable, chaotic, and out of control. We may begin to question the worldview that previously offered us a sense of safety, control, and comfort. We may question God, Scripture as a trusted guide for life, goodness in the world, and an ultimate meaning and purpose for life. Gradually, these enduring, often unanswerable questions that focus on the cause of our trauma-based suffering can give rise to problematic forms of rumination.

When we ruminate, we may continue to dwell on a past event or current emotion.[55] We may do so in an overly abstract, analytical manner. When we overthink in this way, we are disconnected from what we are physiologically feeling, emotions-wise, in the body. We are lost in our head, not connected to our moment-by-moment feelings and physical sensations. We may be preoccupied with the causes or consequences of a traumatic event,[56] along with our symptoms. However, rather than successfully processing the trauma-related memories and emotions in a concrete, experiential manner, we may end up relying on overly verbal, language-based thinking. In other words, we end up thinking about, not feeling, our feelings.

Rumination commonly includes asking unanswerable "Why" questions, like "Why did this happen?" rather than process-oriented "How" and "What" questions, such as "How do I feel about this?" and "What am I feeling right now?" We end up functioning as a philosopher or mathematician who thinks when we need to be a poet or artist who feels. Although asking "Why" questions is certainly part of what it means to be human, given we naturally look for meaning in suffering, they may never offer the answers we are looking for. Instead, we may end up perseverating on more abstract questions, which distracts us from living life and prevents us from processing our memories and emotions. Consequence-wise, rumination may increase the intensity of the emotions we are trying to distance ourselves from and get in the way of us solving problems (because we end up being overly pessimistic and too abstract and fail to act).

When we notice we are overly focused on causal preoccupations, we can pivot away from such unanswerable "Why" questions about the causes and consequences[57] of the traumatic event and our trauma symptoms and toward God's attributes (God is infinitely loving/good, wise, powerful, and present), actions (God's providential care), and presence. In other words, we can shift from the source to the process, that is, questioning God to resting in his presence. We can do so because rumination doesn't work, pragmatically speaking. Rather, it chips away at the very worldview we need for safety, stability, and confidence as we navigate a fallen, broken world. Because of this, we need to prioritize a relationship with a trustworthy traveling companion, the Trinitarian God of the Bible, on the uncertain roads of life.

We can make this pivot through various meditative practices that are housed within the centuries-old Christian tradition, rather than relying on Buddhist mindfulness meditation. These practices, introduced briefly in Chapter 1, offer us the same mental skills of attention, focus on the present moment, awareness, and acceptance[58] that Buddhist mindfulness offers to ameliorate trauma-based rumination and other trauma symptoms. Yet, we are cultivating these skills by drawing from our own Christian, not an unfamiliar Buddhist, religious heritage. Although these historic Christian practices will be unpacked in more detail in a step-by-step manner in the subsequent skill-based chapters, for now, I'd like to discuss them in the context of a Christian understanding of trauma-based suffering. This discussion will provide a rationale for why I have chosen them to help you in your trauma-based suffering in subsequent chapters of this workbook.

Pivoting Toward God's Promises[59]

Within the Protestant tradition, the Puritans were English Christians who lived in the 1500s and 1600s. They wrote a wide variety of enduring Christian classics to help us apply a Christian worldview to all of life. One such collection of works focused on God's promises to us found in Scripture.

Throughout the Bible, we read about God's assurances that he will carry out certain plans. Whereas humans inevitably fail to deliver on our promises because we are fallen human beings, God is trustworthy. We can trust in God's promises because he is infinitely good/loving, wise, powerful, and present. He wants what is best for us, knows all possible scenarios, and has the power and presence to carry out the best plan for our lives. God's promises reveal his benevolent intentions for us. Although they have not been fully carried out because they extend into the future, we can trust that he will do so because of who he is. For example, in Isaiah 41:10, we read, "So do not fear, for I am with you; do not be dismayed, for I am your God. I will strengthen you and help you; I will uphold you with my righteous right hand."

In the context of trauma-related suffering, after a traumatic event, we may begin to question whether this world is safe, predictable, and certain. We may question God's goodness, wisdom, power, and presence. We may question the Christian worldview that previously brought us certainty, confidence, and comfort. We may begin to ruminate on unanswerable "Why" questions that only leave us stuck and prevent us from processing the traumatic event in helpful ways. When we begin to focus our attention on ruminative "Why" questions that chisel away at our worldview, we can gently shift our attention toward God's promises. We can decide what we choose to ruminate on. If rumination, more broadly, is simply repetitive thought, we can repetitively think about God's promises, not dwell on the causes and consequence of the traumatic event.[60] We can prioritize being with God as we meditate on his promises, not get stuck in questioning him as the source of the traumatic event. If God's promises emphasize his goodness carried out in the future, we can place our hope in him, rather than getting overwhelmed with speculative "Why" questions.

Pivoting Toward the Presence of God[61]

Within the Catholic Christian tradition, Brother Lawrence lived in a French monastery in the 1600s. He was apparently a humble man who lived a simple life. He developed a reputation for practicing the presence of God in all of life, even when engaging in what we might consider mundane activities like washing dishes.

But what does it mean to practice the presence of God? It means to recognize that God is active and present in each unfolding moment. It is to recognize his presence as we move through life, whether engaging in important or inconsequential activities. It is to begin to see that God is at the center, not on the periphery, of our reality.

In the context of traumatic events and trauma-based rumination, practicing God's presence can help us to stay rooted in the present moment, rather than ruminating about the causes or consequences of the event in a perseverative manner. In other words, we can emphasize a functional, not causal, perspective on our trauma-related suffering. By spending time with God in the present moment, not ruminating about the past with often unanswerable "Why" questions, we can accomplish at least two main goals.

First, we are letting go of ruminating about the past (given the traumatic event is done) or worrying about the future (since only God knows what the future will hold). Second, we are prioritizing an experience, not abstract thought. In other words, we are cultivating a real relationship with a real God in the here-and-now, not getting lost in analytical thinking about "Why" questions that may never produce satisfying answers. As we learn to anchor ourselves to the present moment, where God is ministering to us, we can find safety and comfort in our relationship with him.

Pivoting Toward the Name of Jesus[62]

Within the Orthodox Christian tradition, Christian monks from the 4th to 15th centuries documented their psychological and spiritual insights into the human experience. They were especially interested in offering teachings on their relationship with God to impact positive psychological and spiritual change.

One such practice was the Jesus Prayer. The long version is "Lord Jesus Christ, Son of God, have mercy on me, a sinner," whereas the short version is "Lord Jesus Christ, have mercy on me." The prayer was likely inspired by people asking Jesus for mercy, or loving-kindness and healing, in the gospels.[63] It may also be based on the Apostle Paul's instruction to "Pray without ceasing."[64]

With this famous prayer, we are learning to become more aware of the inner world, including the thoughts that may pull us away from God. These tempting, compulsive thoughts (with themes of pride, anger, and greed, among others) can distract us from fellowshipping with God. When we are not watchful of our inner world, we may end up ruminating on unhelpful content, which undermines the intimacy with God we long for.

One 19th century Orthodox writer, Theophan the Recluse, put it this way:

> Make it your habit to pray these words with your mind in your heart: "Lord Jesus Christ, Son of God, have mercy on me." And this prayer, when you have learned to use it properly, or rather, when it becomes grafted to your heart, will lead you to the end which you desire: it will unite your mind with your heart, it will quell the turbulence of your thoughts, and it will give you power to govern the movements of your soul.[65]

So, this prayer, when prayed regularly, can help us ruminate on the right things, or thing for that matter—Jesus Christ. We are also uniting our mind and our heart, rather than staying lost in ruminative thoughts. When we practice the prayer, also called the "Prayer of the Heart," we are imagining that we are calling on the name of Jesus in our heart, where he is dwelling. By doing this, we are holistically integrating what we are thinking and feeling. This contrasts with overly relying on an analytical, abstract mind.

When considering trauma-related rumination, the Jesus Prayer can help us to get to know the inner world with greater awareness. We are learning to notice ruminative thinking that is unproductive and pulls us away from communion with God. With the Jesus Prayer, we are ruminating on God, not trauma-based content. This productive form of rumination helps us to rest in his presence as we "unite mind and heart," rather than getting stuck in more abstract, analytical, perseverative thinking that can make trauma symptoms worse. We are also inviting God to be with us in our inner world. With Jesus dwelling within, we need not be afraid of intrusive memories and distressing emotions. We also need not resort to rumination as a cognitive avoidance strategy or the pursuit of causal explanations for trauma-based suffering. When Jesus is present, his mercy, or loving-kindness, is enough.

Pivoting Toward "Finding God in All Things"[66]

Within the Jesuit Christian tradition, one saying is quite popular: "Find God in all things." This saying means that we are to ask how God is active and moving in our daily lives, not just when we are worshipping on Sunday morning at church. By accepting God's presence moment by moment, we are better able to find comfort in his loving presence and discern his will throughout the day. We can recognize all the distractions that pull us away from God. We can choose to be more like Christ as we fellowship with him.

In *Spiritual Exercises*, the 16th century Jesuit Ignatius of Loyola offered a variety of psychological and spiritual strategies to draw closer to God and rest in his loving care. Originally developed as a sort of manual for a four-week spiritual retreat, *Spiritual Exercises* consists of prayer- and meditation-based practices with step-by-step instructions. These practices are meant to better understand our thinking and feeling and relationship with God. Overall, they help us to see that God is active in both our inner and outer world.

One such practice, the daily examen, helps us to look back on our day, then the next day ahead, to discern God's presence. As we examine our day, we are trying to recognize and accept God's presence in both our inner and outer world. Within the Christian life, we are attempting to identify both "consolations" (that is, pleasant thoughts, feelings, and behaviors that move us toward God) and "desolations" (that is, unpleasant thoughts, feelings, and behaviors that move us away from God) and God's activity in and through them. Although we may automatically think of consolations as from God and desolations as from the Devil, God may allow desolations to help us learn to endure, get our attention, or remind us of the need for his grace and dependence on him. Therefore, the daily examen helps us to accept *all* our daily experiences, whether pleasant or unpleasant, with patience. As we accept them, we are learning to ask what God is up to during them. This contrasts with merely accepting pleasant experiences and trying to avoid unpleasant ones.

In the context of trauma-based symptoms, rumination is often employed as a cognitive avoidance strategy to distance ourselves from trauma-based intrusive memories and distressing emotions. As an antidote, the daily examen can help us to "Find God in all things." This means we can learn to accept God's loving presence amid our inner struggles, rather than trying to avoid them through rumination. Given avoidance doesn't work, we can lovingly accept God's comfort during our times of need. By doing this, we can allow the intrusive memories and distressing emotions to run their natural course. We can recognize they are impermanent and, thus, need not harm us. If God is dwelling within, we need not fear our trauma symptoms. Accepting, not avoiding, our trauma symptoms can also be useful for pragmatic purposes— ruminative avoidance may make our trauma symptoms worse. Overall, with the daily examen, we are learning to recognize that God is dwelling within, even during our most difficult experiences of trauma-based suffering.

Taken together, the Protestant, Catholic, and Orthodox traditions can offer us a plethora of psychological and spiritual strategies to respond to trauma symptoms more effectively. These strategies can help us shift our attention from rumination to God, practice God's presence in the here-and-now in response to rumination, cultivate awareness of rumination by calling on the name of Jesus, and move toward the acceptance of unpleasant memories and emotions by inviting God to be with us in them. Let's now turn to two exercises to help you better understand your own views on trauma-based suffering and engage in a simple activity to pivot from focusing on the causal "Why" to functional "How" of God during trauma-based suffering.

Exercises

Exploring Personal Views of Trauma-Based Suffering[67]

For this first of two exercises in the chapter, I'd like for you to begin to identify your own views of trauma-based suffering. Drawing upon the previous list, see if you can spend some time journaling about what types of views of trauma-related suffering you have, where they came from, and whether they are causal or functional. Remember, with causal views, we typically try to identify the source (like God) and the source's contribution toward the trauma-based suffering. We may do so with "Why" questions, like "Why did you allow this, God?" On the other hand, with functional views, we often emphasize the purpose/plan/outcome. We prioritize "What" questions, like "What purpose/plan/ outcome do you have for me, God?" Please use extra paper if needed.

1. What views of suffering do you tend to believe in or gravitate toward? Why?

   _____

   _____

   _____

   _____

   _____

   _____

2. When did these views begin to develop? When do you first remember believing in them?

_____

_____

_____

_____

_____

_____

_____

3. What traumatic events have shaped these views of suffering?

_____

_____

_____

_____

_____

_____

4. Do these views of suffering tend to be causal (with "Why" questions) or functional (with "What" and "How" questions)?

_____

_____

_____

_____

_____

_____

5. What impact do these views of suffering have on your trauma symptoms, including trauma-based rumination?

    _____

    _____

    _____

    _____

    _____

    _____

6. What impact do these views of suffering have on your relationship with God?

    _____

    _____

    _____

    _____

    _____

    _____

7. If you tend to gravitate toward more causal views, what might it be like to shift toward more functional views? How might this shift impact your trauma symptoms, including trauma-based rumination? How might this shift impact your relationship with God?

    _____

    _____

    _____

    _____

    _____

    _____

Pivoting from a Causal to Functional View of Suffering[68]

Now I'd like us to build on the previous journaling exercise and the last chapter's exercise of non-judgmentally noticing the inner and outer world. Specifically, I'd like us to spend this time shifting from a causal view to a functional view of suffering by simply practicing God's presence. Rather than asking God "Why" questions in response to traumatic events and struggling to believe in God's infinite goodness, wisdom, power, presence, and providential care, my hope is that we can simply spend this time with him by resting in his loving presence. Our aim is to ask God what he is up to and where he is leading us in response to the traumatic event and trauma-related symptoms.

Find a quiet location, free from distractions. Sit up straight in a supportive chair with your eyes closed. When you are ready, start by turning to your inner world. This will be followed by noticing your outer world. Adding to the last chapter's exercise, we'll be inviting God to be with us in this moment. He is with us in the inner world and outer world right here and right now.

1. Simply become aware of, from a place of non-judgmental awareness and acceptance, what you are experiencing with your thoughts, feelings, sensations, memories, and images. What are you thinking right now? Feeling? Sensing? Remembering? Imagining? Just notice these psychological experiences without needing to do anything with them.

2. Invite God to be with you in your thoughts, feelings, sensations, memories, and images. You may want to say a simple phrase to capture your openness to God's activity in the here-and-now, such as "Welcome, God." Welcome God into your thoughts. Welcome God into your feelings. Welcome God into your sensations. Welcome God into your memories. Welcome God into your images. Because he is with you right now, dwelling within, there is nothing else you need to do. You can just let these inner experiences—thoughts, feelings, sensations, memories, and images—run their natural course without trying to change them in any way, with God dwelling within.

3. Use your God-given sense of sight to notice five things in the room. Try not to judge this experience. Instead, just notice five things with an open curiosity. Like last chapter, you may notice the walls around you, carpet or flooring beneath your feet, furniture that takes up space in the room, or paintings hanging on the walls.

4. Invite God to be with you in this moment as you notice your environment around you with your God-given sense of sight. Recognize that God is with you in this very moment. He's dwelling within,

and he's also with you in the room. Because God is omnipresent, meaning he's everywhere at once, he is spending this time with you. Even though nothing exciting is happening right now, God is still spending this time with you. Don't try to change this moment in any way. Instead, just notice five things in the room, with God dwelling all around you.

This exercise was meant to help you begin to shift from trauma-based rumination to Christian attention, focus on the present moment, awareness, and acceptance,[69] which we'll practice in subsequent chapters. Before concluding the chapter, I'd like to share a case to help you better understand a Christian view of suffering and what to do about it, anchored to a Christian worldview.

Case Example

Arabella grew up in a small town in the Midwest region of the United States. After college, she married a Christian man who she met and fell in love with during her college years. Wanting to start a family, her husband, John, got a job at a large company in a coastal city so she could stay at home with the kids. Over the next few years, they had three children, two boys and a girl.

Gradually, they got plugged in to a local church and built a church community. Arabella and John attended church every Sunday morning, volunteered in several ministries, and coached their kids' sports. Everything was going well until one traumatizing evening.

Arabella got a phone call on her cell phone when she was at home with the kids. It was a weekday afternoon, and the police called to tell her that her husband just died. Although they gave no other details over the phone, they asked her to come down to the hospital to answer some questions.

Quickly getting into the car, dropping off the kids at a neighbor's house, and heading to the hospital, Arabella was overwhelmed with fear, anxiety, sadness, and doubt. She didn't know how to cope with the incredible sense of confusion she was going through. As she got to the hospital, everything was a blur. A police officer told her that her husband had taken his own life. When she heard this, she was in utter shock. Hadn't they built a good life together? Wasn't God at the center of their lives? Didn't they attend church, go to a small group, attend weekly Bible studies, and serve in ministries?

Heading home, she didn't know what to do. How would she tell her children? Where was God in all of this? Was there a God? Her sense of safety, predictability, and control quickly vanished. The world, almost instantly, seemed like an alien planet that she had no familiarity with.

That night while in bed, she had vivid images of her husband's last moments. She felt overwhelmed with sadness, loneliness, and fear, which she wanted to avoid at all costs. How would she endure this overwhelming pain? In response to the distressing memories and emotions, she began to ruminate.

Why did God allow this to happen? Why didn't God intervene to help John? Was God punishing her in some way? Was God good like the Bible said he was? How could a loving God allow so much suffering now? Was God even real at all? Her mind kept going around in circles, with no satisfying answers.

Over the next few weeks, she received tremendous support from family and her church community. Several family members moved in with her to help her with the kids. Pastors visited her at her home to pray with her. She felt a deep sense of appreciation toward all the people who selflessly responded to her needs.

Yet, she continued to ruminate most of the day. This led to her pastor suggesting that she see a local Christian counselor, Dr. Smith. Dr. Smith graduated from a local Christian university and was a licensed professional counselor. He also had seminary training, including a background in Christian spiritual practices.

Working together, Dr. Smith helped Arabella begin to process the pain she was feeling. He helped her express her fear, anxiety, loneliness, and sadness. She was able to verbalize these emotions to him in counseling and to God via lament. He also helped her to see that the loss of her husband, John, was deeply traumatizing for her. Dr. Smith explained that, although lament is a healthy way to cry out to God, her rumination, when engaged in for prolonged periods of time, might be a way to distance herself from images of John's last moments and the corresponding emotions she felt.

Arabella shared with Dr. Smith that her rumination never left her feeling safe or at peace, and she was mentally exhausted. In response, Dr. Smith taught her a simple Christian spiritual practice of noticing her rumination, then shifting toward an awareness of God's loving presence.[70] To make this pivot, Dr. Smith worked with Arabella to identify a short phrase that helped her to rest in God's love, not continue to dwell on the causal "Why" questions that left her stuck. The phrase, taken from Psalm 46:10, was "Be still." Whenever she started to ruminate, she would gently repeat this phrase to remind her that God was with her. Although she didn't know why John's life was lost, she could rest in God's presence to find needed comfort and peace.

Over the next several months, Arabella and Dr. Smith would explore many more of her thoughts, emotions, and beliefs about suffering and John's passing. Still, this two-step process of noticing and shifting helped her to gain some stability during an overwhelming time. Arabella could find comfort in her relationship with God, even though God's providence was a mystery.

Conclusion

To conclude this chapter, a Christian worldview offers an understanding of who God is, God's activity in the world, suffering, and the purpose of suffering. In fact, there are many views of suffering within the Christian tradition. When traumatic events take place, our worldview may be questioned, and we may begin to ruminate with "Why" questions. Rumination may be pursued to distance ourselves from difficult memories and emotions in an overly analytical, abstract manner. Still, rumination may end up making the very symptoms we are trying to avoid worse. This is because we need to process the trauma-related memories and emotions, feeling what there is to feel. Because of this, we may wish to shift from more causal views of suffering (which emphasize God as the source) to more functional views (which prioritize God's loving presence, plan, and purpose).[71] By doing this, we can begin to practice God's presence to move through trauma-based suffering with a trustworthy, loving traveling companion who works things out for good.[72]

To shift from trauma-based rumination and "Why" questions to practicing God's presence, the Christian tradition offers many practices. These practices can serve as a Christian-sensitive alternative to Buddhist mindfulness to develop the needed mental skills of attention, focus on the present moment, awareness, and acceptance.[73] In fact, I've researched these Christian skills and practices with a four-week intervention, which I've expanded to form this very workbook. In the next chapter, I'll be offering an introduction to this four-skill approach, which is anchored to a Christian worldview and psychological and spiritual practices. From there, the remaining four chapters will focus on each of the four skills so you can shift from trauma-based rumination to God.

Notes

1 Janoff-Bulman (1992).
2 See, for example, John 3:16.
3 Philippians 2:6–11.
4 Romans 4:25; 1 Corinthians 15:12–19.
5 Romans 10:9.
6 2 Corinthians 5:18–19.
7 See Genesis 21.
8 Hebrews 4:15.
9 Hebrews 4:16.
10 Romans 5:8.
11 See, for example, Anderson et al. (2017) for a comprehensive review of a Christian worldview. In the psychology literature, see Knabb et al. (2019b, 2025) for a better understanding of a Christian worldview from a psychological perspective.

12 Romans 8:39; Ephesians 3:18–19.
13 Psalm 147:5; Romans 11:33.
14 Psalm 147:5; Jeremiah 32:17; Isaiah 40:28.
15 Psalm 139:7–10.
16 Psalm 66:7; Psalm 103.19; Matthew 5:45.
17 Romans 8:28.
18 2 Corinthians 4:18; Ephesians 2:6; Ephesians 6:12.
19 Revelation 21:4.
20 Psalm 119:105.
21 2 Timothy 3:16.
22 Exodus 20.
23 Matthew 5–7.
24 Galatians 5:22–23.
25 Colossians 3:2.
26 Romans 8:35.
27 Western Shorter Catechism (1648). See also, e.g., Psalm 86:12 and Revelation 4:11.
28 Knabb and Wang (2021).
29 Knabb et al. (2025).
30 Knabb et al. (2017).
31 Janoff-Bulman (1992).
32 Lament psalms include those found in Psalm 6 and 22. Within these psalms of lament, we see questions (including "Why" questions) directed to God to process painful human experiences. See also Brueggemann (1985) for a review of the psalms for different seasons of life, including the lament psalms for seasons of disorientation, sadness, and other types of pain and turmoil.
33 APA (2022).
34 Hall and Hill (2019).
35 Janoff-Bulman (1992).
36 Janoff-Bulman (1992, p. 6).
37 Flavel (2022).
38 Pew Research Center (2021).
39 This list is based on a review of McMartin and Hall (2022), the Stanford Encyclopedia of Philosophy (2024), and Scripture.
40 Romans 5:12.
41 Isaiah 63:9.
42 Philippians 3:10.
43 2 Corinthians 1:4.
44 1 Peter 4:15–16.
45 1 Peter 1:7; 1 Peter 4:12.
46 Job 13:15.
47 Romans 5:3–5.
48 Romans 8:28.
49 Hebrews 12:6.
50 McMartin and Hall (2022).
51 McMartin and Hall (2022).
52 McMartin and Hall (2022).
53 McMartin and Hall (2022).
54 Hall and Hill (2019).

55 This paragraph is based on a review of Ehlers and Steil (1995), Ehring et al. (2009), and Watkins and Roberts (2020).

56 Ehlers and Clark (2000).

57 Ehlers and Clark (2000).

58 Feldman et al. (2007).

59 This review of God's promises is based on Beeke and Jones' (2012) chapter on "The Puritans on Understanding and Using God's Promises."

60 Ehlers and Clark (2000).

61 This review of Brother Lawrence is based on Lawrence (2015).

62 This review of the *Philokalia* and Jesus Prayer is based on Coniaris (1998) and Nikodimos (1782).

63 Mark 10:47.

64 1 Thessalonians 5:17.

65 Quoted in Coniaris (1998, Location No. 1564).

66 This review is based on Ignatian Spirituality (n.d.b), Gallagher (2006), and Ivens (1998).

67 This exercise is based in part on a review of McMartin and Hall (2022).

68 This exercise is based in part on a review of Harris' (2019) "Dropping Anchor" exercise, Lawrence (2015), and McMartin and Hall (2022).

69 Feldman et al. (2007); Knabb et al. (2022).

70 Knabb (2021).

71 McMartin and Hall (2022).

72 Romans 8:28.

73 Feldman et al. (2007).

Trauma

A Four-Skill Integrative Approach

Introduction

For Chapter 4, I'll first introduce you to the general background, theme, and goals for the approach in this workbook to pave the way for the four specific skill-based chapters. I'll then offer empirical support and practical considerations. The practical considerations include the ideal time commitment (the minutes and days for each exercise) and setting. I'll also provide encouragement and a prayer to prepare you for the four-skill journey ahead.

Background

Within the Christian tradition, Christian writers differentiate between God's common and special grace. God's common grace refers to the undeserved gifts that God, in his goodness and mercy, provides humankind even though we are fallen and sinful.[1] These gifts may include unique and extraordinary talents and skills. They may also include the ability for scientists to make scientific discoveries. And they may include secular psychologists' insights into the human mind and behavior. So, when it comes to trauma research, Christians can benefit from secular psychologists' understanding that trauma-based rumination is a cognitive avoidance strategy that may increase the frequency

DOI: 10.4324/9781003647270-4

and intensity of the intrusive memories and emotions we are trying to distance ourselves from.[2] Christians can also benefit from at least some of the good that comes from mindfulness and mindfulness-based practices. Indeed, even Christians can be aided by research that reveals the mental skills of attention, focus on the present moment, awareness, and acceptance can be helpful for psychological health.[3]

In contrast, special grace captures the undeserved merit, favor, and blessings that God offers only to Christians to redeem and sanctify us.[4] Because the Holy Spirit dwells within upon giving our life to Christ, Christians can become more like Christ in our thoughts, feelings, and behaviors. If sanctification is simply defined as becoming holy and more like Jesus Christ within both our inner and outer world, God's special grace allows Christians to become more like him, psychologically and spiritually, on a daily basis.

Combined, God's common and special grace means Christians can benefit from *both* secular psychological science *and* our own Christian tradition to ameliorate psychological suffering and become more like Christ in the process. This integrated understanding is the foundation for the current workbook. Because traumatic events can cause so much psychological turmoil, Christians can look to at least some secular insights within the scientific discipline of psychology. We can do so by drawing upon empirical findings that don't contradict our Christian worldview in any way. Yet, as Christians, we recognize that our relationship with Christ is paramount for healing and change. Because of this, both common and special grace can be harnessed in the promotion of Christian mental and spiritual health.

Overall, I believe Trinitarian mental health involves being empowered by the Holy Spirit to walk with the Son home to the Father. On this side of heaven, the Holy Spirit offers us comfort as he dwells within. As the Holy Spirit dwells within, we walk with Jesus Christ, the Son, who understands our weaknesses because he was fully human.[5] Jesus loves us to the point of offering us a plan to be reconciled to God. As we walk with Jesus along the roads of life, we have a destination ahead. We will one day be face-to-face with God in heaven, where there will be no more suffering. Eventually, God will create a new heaven and earth. Thus, we have hope in the future, even though we experience trauma-related suffering in the present. This perspective helps us to respond to suffering with needed wisdom—trauma-related suffering is certainly difficult, but it is temporary, and we have a trustworthy traveling companion to see us home.

Theme and Goals

With the above foundation in mind, the main theme of this workbook comes from Colossians 3:1–2: "Since, then, you have been raised with Christ, set your hearts on things above, where Christ is, seated at the right hand of God. Set your minds on things above, not on earthly things." With this passage, we see that Christians are to focus on an eternal, heavenly reality, not be preoccupied by a temporary, earthly reality.[6]

In the context of traumatic events and trauma-related suffering, we are learning to recognize that Christ is with us in our suffering. We are by no means left to endure our suffering alone. Rather, Jesus understands our suffering.[7] After all, he is the Suffering Servant.[8] Because he understands us and is with us in our pain, we can focus our mind on him, not the rumination that keeps us stuck in life. We can ruminate in a healthy way on God's Word, not our own inaccurate content from our own fallen human mind. Essentially, we are always ruminating or mentally chewing on something. The question is whether we are ruminating on cognitive material that is healthy or unhealthy for us. Are we trusting in God or "leaning on our own understanding?"[9] Our own self-generated content of the mind can be distorted, given our imperfect human mind is faulty.[10] However, Christians consider scriptural content to be God's revealed truth. It can be used for "teaching, rebuking, correcting, and training in righteousness."[11]

A biological parallel may be helpful here. As humans, we need to eat food daily for our physical health. Yet, we have a choice. We can choose to eat food that nourishes us and contributes to a healthy lifestyle or junk food that leads to weight gain, clogged arteries, and other medical issues. In a similar vein, we can choose to ruminate, or meditate, on thoughts that contribute to either mental health or dysfunction. This program will help you shift from unhealthy to healthy forms of rumination, with God at the center to see us through.

Building on this foundation, the four major goals of the four-skill program are as follows:[12]

1. To understand the link between trauma-related intrusive memories, emotions, and rumination.
2. To understand the role that a distinctly Christian form of meditation (with the four skills of Christian attention, Christian focus on the present moment, Christian awareness, and Christian acceptance) can play in helping you shift from unhealthy trauma-based rumination to healthy rumination on God.
3. To learn about the role that Christian meditation and prayer, drawn from Puritan, Catholic, Orthodox, and Jesuit sources within Christianity, can play in helping you develop the above four skills to shift from unhealthy trauma-based rumination to healthy rumination on God.
4. To practice Puritan meditation to cultivate Christian attention, the presence of God to cultivate Christian focus on the present moment, the Jesus Prayer to cultivate Christian awareness, and the daily

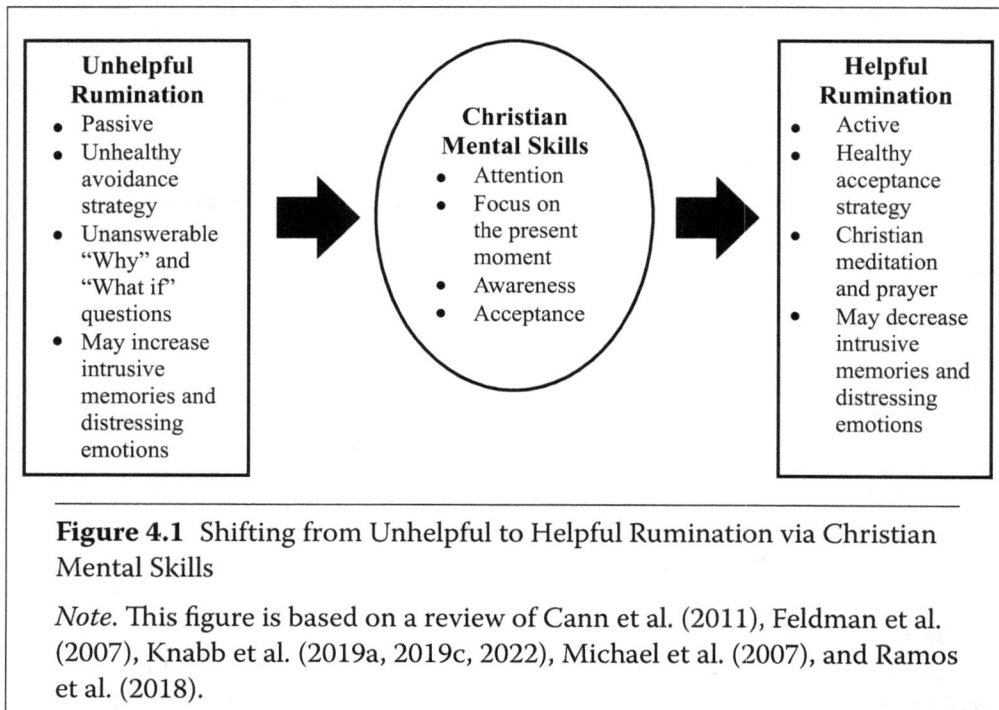

Figure 4.1 Shifting from Unhelpful to Helpful Rumination via Christian Mental Skills

Note. This figure is based on a review of Cann et al. (2011), Feldman et al. (2007), Knabb et al. (2019a, 2019c, 2022), Michael et al. (2007), and Ramos et al. (2018).

examen to cultivate Christian acceptance to shift from unhealthy trauma-based rumination to healthy rumination on God.

To offer a visual reminder of this process, see Figure 4.1, which was already presented in Chapter 1.

As revealed in Figure 4.1, to successfully shift from unhealthy trauma-based rumination to healthy rumination on God, the four mental skills can be helpful. We'll be focusing on one mental skill per chapter moving forward. I've personally researched this approach in two empirical studies, described next.

Empirical Support

This four-skill manual is based on two empirical studies, first introduced in Chapter 1. For the first study, I worked with two colleagues to develop and test a theoretical understanding of the relationship between trauma-based rumination, mindful skills, and focusing on God among a Christian sample of trauma survivors.[13] With a sample of online Christian adults who reported a history of traumatic experiences, we investigated the relationship between these variables. Almost one in three participants in the study reported experiencing a natural disaster, almost one in two reported being in a car accident, and one in two reported experiencing the death of a loved one, among other traumatic events.

Regarding rumination, we asked participants the following question: "What do you do when memories of the traumatic event pop into your mind?" In response to this question, they were given several items to rate from "never" to "always," including "I think about how life would have been different if the event had not occurred" and "I dwell on what I should have done differently."[14] Participants were also asked about religious and/or spiritual content when they ruminate with the following question: "When you think about the traumatic event, how frequently do you dwell on the following thoughts?" Different options included "God turned away from me," "God abandoned me," and "God neglected me."[15] In addition, we asked participants how often they lived out four mindful skills: attention, focus on the present moment, awareness, and acceptance.[16] Finally, we asked participants how often they focused their mind on religious content (e.g., prayer, God) to cope with traumatic events.

Results revealed that Christian rumination was negatively associated with mindful skills, which was positively associated with focusing on God. In other words, as the Christian trauma survivors reported less rumination (that is, dwelling on what they could have done differently in response to the traumatic event, dwelling on God's neglect or absence surrounding the traumatic event), they reported they were more likely to utilize the four skills of attention, focus on the present moment, awareness, and acceptance in life. And as they reported greater mindful skills, they reported greater efforts to focus on God in response to traumatic events. These results offered us empirical support for the theoretical notion that Christian trauma survivors can pivot from trauma-based rumination to ruminating (that is, focusing) on God. With these results in mind, we turned to investigating a four-week intervention for Christian trauma survivors.

For the second study, I worked with several colleagues to develop and test a four-week program for Christian trauma survivors to shift from trauma-based rumination to ruminating on God.[17] To be included in the intervention, participants needed to have a history of traumatic events and struggling with unwanted memories about the event and rumination in response to the event. We administered the four-week intervention online to two different samples, first to a sample of Christian college students, then to a sample of Christian community adults. Each week, participants learned and practiced a separate Christian meditative or prayer practice to cultivate a skill: Week 1 emphasized the skill of attention with Puritan meditation, Week 2 emphasized the skill of focus on the present moment with the practice of the presence of God, Week 3 emphasized the skill of awareness with the Jesus Prayer, and Week 4 emphasized the skill of acceptance with the daily examen. We measured trauma-based rumination (with themes concerning both the event itself and

God), mindful skills (attention, focus on the present moment, awareness, and acceptance), focusing on God in response to traumatic events, and trauma symptoms during two time periods: prior to the start of Week 1 and at the conclusion of Week 4.

For the sample of Christian college students, pre- to post-intervention, the intervention group that practiced Christian meditation and prayer reported less trauma-based rumination (with themes surrounding both the event itself and God) and other trauma symptoms and greater mindful skills (attention, focus on the present moment, awareness, and acceptance) and efforts to focus on God. With the sample of Christian community adults, the findings were mostly the same. Pre- to post-intervention, the intervention group that practiced Christian meditation and prayer reported less trauma-based rumination (this time surrounding only the event itself) and other trauma symptoms and greater mindful skills (attention, focus on the present moment, awareness, and acceptance). Overall, these results across two Christian samples of trauma survivors suggest that the four-skill approach in this workbook can be helpful for pivoting from trauma-based rumination to ruminating on God via attention, focus on the present moment, awareness, and acceptance. When this pivot happens, we may be able to reduce other trauma symptoms, too. Let's now move on to practical considerations so you can begin to prepare for the four-skill approach offered in the next four chapters.

Practical Considerations

Time Commitment

In terms of the time commitment, a recent study[18] on mindfulness-based practices compared three different groups: a group that practiced for four 20-minute sessions over a two-week period, a group that practiced for four 5-minute sessions over a two-week period, and a group that was instructed to just listen to an audiobook for two weeks (as a control group). Results revealed that both the 20-minute and 5-minute groups reported an increase in mindfulness (e.g., present-moment awareness and acceptance) and a decrease in the symptoms of depression, anxiety, and stress. However, the 5-minute group reported a greater increase in mindfulness and a greater decrease in stress than the 20-minute group.

With these results in mind, I suggest setting aside 10 minutes for each of the activities in the next four chapters. This way, you'll be able to settle into each practice, but you won't devote so much time each day that you get burned out or struggle to implement the practices daily. And there may be no added benefit if you practice more than 10 minutes per day.

Regarding the number of days in a row that you should practice each exercise, in the above four-week intervention study, the Christian trauma survivors were instructed to practice each exercise daily for a week. Although I don't necessarily offer specific guidance in the current workbook on how many days in a row you should practice per exercise, you may want to consider spending a week at a time in each of the next four chapters, consistent with the original study. Then, once you are familiar with each exercise, you can attempt to integrate them long-term into daily life.

Setting

In consideration of the setting, I'd suggest an environment that is quiet and free from noise and other sensory distractions. Silence can be extremely important for meditative and prayer practices. It can allow us to turn inward to get to know the full range of psychological experiences we are having. These experiences include our thinking patterns and what we are feeling and remembering. Silence can also have a calming and settling effect. Although silence may seem scary at first for trauma survivors, it can help us to relate differently to our inner world, which is a hoped-for outcome with the four mental skills presented in this workbook. Interestingly, Christian monks throughout the ages have written on the importance of silence in meditative and contemplative practices to commune with God.[19] Outer silence, from this perspective, can lead to inner silence. And this inner silence can help to calm and settle an overly ruminative mind that is shouting at us and demanding our attention.

In addition to finding a quiet environment, I'd suggest trying to remain physically still in a supportive, comfortable chair (except for the walking exercise in Chapter 6). Try to find a chair that allows you to sit up straight, with good posture if you can sit in an erect, upright position. Returning to Christian monastic writings, Christian monks have long taught that outer stillness can lead to inner stillness.[20] So, combined, outer silence and stillness can help us with inner silence and stillness. And this inner silence and stillness can be helpful for responding to trauma-based rumination.

One author uses the metaphor of a pond, which has been used in Christian monastic writings to capture the importance of silence and stillness for the soul.[21] With a pond, the surrounding winds may agitate the water, to the point that the water is murky. When the water is muddy due to the surrounding winds, we can't see through the water to the bottom of the pond. Yet, when the wind calms and pond settles, we can clearly see to the bottom. So, conditions outside of the pond can impact what goes on under the pond's surface. Likewise, when we practice outer silence and stillness, we are in a better position for the soul within to settle. In turn, we can clearly see into the depths of our being, where God dwells within. We gain insight and clarity into the inner world, rather than remaining confused and agitated. Let's now shift to a word of encouragement and closing prayer, which will be followed by the four skill-based chapters.

Encouragement and Prayer

In the last decade or so, as a Christian psychologist, I've been especially fascinated with a New Testament word. In Greek, it is *hupomone*. It is commonly presented as patience in English translations of the New Testament of the Bible. However, I don't think this translation is completely accurate. *Hupomone* is more fully a hopeful, faithful, patient, courageous endurance and perseverance.[22] It is a virtue that captures psychological and spiritual stamina in the midst of suffering. In addition to being used in the New Testament, the word was used to depict the experience of early Christian martyrs in the first few centuries after Jesus lived.[23] These Christian martyrs were marched to the Roman Colosseum to be executed for their faith. They needed a faithful, courageous endurance, *hupomone*, to not renounce their faith in God as they faced death. To the very end, they needed to hold on to the hope they had in Christ.

Now, in no way am I suggesting you are going to be marched to a modern-day Colosseum. Rather, my prayer for you is that you maintain faith and hope in the God who will see you through your present psychological suffering. This God knows what it means to suffer, and he's walking with you through your suffering right now. My prayer is that the God of the Bible will give you peace and comfort as you practice the skills in the next four chapters. Although your trauma-based symptoms may never *fully* go away on this side of heaven, God is with you as you learn to shift from unhelpful to helpful forms of rumination. With the above in mind, here is my heartfelt prayer for you, a Christian trauma survivor:

God, I pray that you help this reader endure with hope and courage. May you provide comfort amid suffering and confidence amid confusion. May you help the reader to pivot from their own limited, finite understanding to trusting in you as infinitely loving, wise, powerful, and present, especially during times of uncertainty, doubt, and pain. May the reader increasingly trust in your providential care as you walk with them along the roads of life to reach their eventual destination—to someday, after a long and fruitful life, be face-to-face with you in heaven.

Conclusion

To wrap up this chapter, we have discussed God's common and special grace, along with the theme and goals for this skills-based approach. We've also reviewed the empirical support and practical considerations for the content of this workbook. Next, we will be heading into the four skill-based chapters to practice shifting from unhealthy, human forms of rumination to healthy, biblical forms of rumination.

Notes

1 Treier (2017).
2 Michael et al. (2007).
3 Feldman et al. (2007).
4 Elwell (2001).
5 Hebrews 4:15.
6 Patzia (1990).
7 Hebrews 4:15.
8 Isaiah 53.
9 Proverbs 3:5–6.
10 As a common example, the memory of eyewitnesses in legal proceedings can be flawed in a variety of ways (see, for example, Junnarkar & Lakhani, 2021).
11 2 Timothy 3:16–17.
12 Knabb et al. (2019c, pp. 2–3).
13 Knabb et al. (2019a).
14 Clohessy and Ehlers (1999); Steil and Ehlers (2000).
15 Wilt et al. (2017).
16 Feldman et al. (2007).
17 Knabb et al. (2022).
18 Strohmaier et al. (2021).
19 Paintner (2012).
20 Talbot (2020).
21 Talbot (2020).
22 Barclay (1974).
23 Heyman (2007); Middleton (2011).

CHAPTER 5

Skill 1

Christian Attention

Introduction

In this first of four skill-based chapters, we'll explore attention as a key skill for shifting from rumination to an intentional focus on God. First, a secular psychological perspective on the role that attention plays in trauma symptoms and trauma-based rumination is discussed. Then, a Christian view on the role that God's promises can play in helping us pivot from unhelpful rumination to the promises that God has revealed to us in his Word, the Bible, is presented. Along the way, definitions, examples, and exercises are offered to help you learn to make this salient shift throughout the day with biblical meditation. To conclude, you will read about a real-life example to better understand how to put this skill into practice in the context of trauma symptoms.

A Secular Psychological Perspective

Within secular psychology, researchers frequently study attention and its role in mental health. Attention can be succinctly defined as the mental effort we devote to focusing on stimuli in our inner or outer world to effectively respond to what's occurring in our immediate environment.[1] In the inner world, we can focus our attention on thoughts, feelings, sensations, memories, or images.

DOI: 10.4324/9781003647270-5

In the outer world, we may focus our attention on people, places, things, or activities.

This human ability to attend can be either focused or open.[2] When focused, our attention is sustained on something particular over time, like reading a book. If open, we devote ourselves to "non-reactive monitoring" of whatever emerges within present moment experience, like noticing what thoughts pop into our head and identifying and labeling their theme ("I'm worrying") without needing to do anything with them.[3] To use a camera metaphor, focused attention is like zooming in on one thing, whereas open attention is like zooming out to see the bigger picture. Both are necessary for healthy psychological functioning.

When it comes to trauma symptoms,[4] we may experience intrusive and vivid memories of a prior traumatic event. These memories can be especially distressing and cause difficult emotions such as fear, anxiety, helplessness, guilt, shame, and anger. This is because the memories and images seem so real, and the human brain perceives them as such. Since we may have been in danger when the original event took place, our mind can convince us that the internal memory is really happening in our external environment. We may believe we are unsafe all over again. This experience can take up all our attention. We may end up compulsively ruminating about what happened leading up to the event, the consequences after the event, and the meaning of the event. We may do so to avoid the difficult memory and corresponding emotions. With rumination, questions such as "Why did this happen to me?" "What if it happens again?" "What did I do to deserve this?" and "Why didn't I do more to prevent this?" can persist. We may end up being exhausted from an overactive mind and distracted from living life. Unfortunately, compulsively ruminating about the event with these "Why" and "What if" questions may never lead to satisfying answers that bring comfort. And this repetitive, perseverative, and compulsive type of thinking may unintentionally increase the frequency and intensity of trauma-based memories and emotions. Instead of experientially processing what happened and how we felt (and currently feel) about it in a healthy way, we can get stuck abstractly dwelling on the causes and consequences of the event.[5]

Yet, not all rumination is inevitably negative if we define it more generally as deep repetitious, meditative thought that takes up all our mental attention. Rumination, more broadly, can simply be a type of cognitive processing. One dictionary entry defines rumination as "the act or process of regurgitating and chewing again previously swallowed food."[6] This is like a cow slowly and deliberately chewing cud in a grassy field on a sunny day to extract vital nutrients. The cow is, essentially, ruminating as a positive, nutrient-extracting activity.[7] Psychologically, this type of rumination can be synonymous with meditation, which is a deliberate act of focusing the mind, when we are intentionally ruminating on the right thing. Rumination can be helpful when we are dwelling on positive material to extract healthy psychological nutrients. When we are ruminating in the best possible way, we are thinking deeply, or meditating, on uplifting cognitive content. We are concentrating on it with all our attention and pondering it in a slow, continuous manner for our psychological benefit.[8]

In agreement, trauma researchers have differentiated between two types of rumination. One is unhelpful, negative, passive, and used to avoid psychological pain, and the other is helpful, positive, active, and used to accept and grow from psychological pain.[9] With the unhelpful type, we may focus on more abstract details surrounding the event (like the previously mentioned "Why" and "What if" questions) in a passive manner in an effort to avoid having to experience the corresponding emotional pain.[10] With the helpful type, we might actively dwell on the positive features like finding meaning after the event or learning from the event in an effort to persevere and grow from the psychological pain.[11] Research has revealed that unhelpful types of rumination are positively linked to posttraumatic stress (PTSD) symptoms.[12] In contrast, helpful rumination is positively related to psychological growth.[13] So, rumination may inevitably be part of the psychological processing that takes place after a traumatic event.[14] But the type of rumination—unhelpful versus helpful—is often key in determining mental health outcomes.

Certain skills can assist us in reducing problematic forms of rumination and, as a result, other symptoms as well. In a study among U.S. college students, researchers found that mindful skills were negatively related to rumination, and rumination was positively related to trauma symptoms.[15] The individuals who endorsed the mindful skills of attention, present-moment awareness, and acceptance were less likely to state they ruminated and, in turn, less likely to report trauma symptoms. This may be because they allowed themselves to process what happened and how they felt about it in a mindful, not avoidant, manner. In another study, adults who received outpatient treatment for depression utilized mindfulness to help with their symptoms.[16] Results revealed that the formal practice of mindfulness meditation, which includes the cultivation of attention, helped to reduce their rumination. In yet another study, researchers taught participants who were struggling with depression both mindfulness meditation and loving-kindness meditation, or LKM.[17] With LKM, which comes from the Buddhist religious tradition, participants are instructed to repeat certain positive mantras[18] to cultivate compassion for themselves and others. These statements may include "May I [or you] be safe," "May I [or you] be at ease," and "May I [or you] be free from suffering." LKM was practiced on its own for 60 minutes a day for a week, then practiced for 15 minutes before the mindfulness-based intervention, which was delivered daily for eight weeks. Results revealed a reduction in both symptoms of depression and rumination among the intervention group.

Attention may play a sizeable role in reducing both rumination and psychological symptoms, including trauma. This may be the case because mindfulness meditation and LKM help those who practice it regulate their attention by shifting from their symptoms to another avenue of awareness (such as one of the five senses or the breath) or a positive mantra. Attentional regulation can take the form of focused attention, where we devote our attention to one thing in the moment. It can also consist of open attention, where we learn to just notice our ruminative mind in a non-reactive way without needing to impulsively react to it.

With mindfulness of the breath, for example, we are invited to simply notice our breath with non-judgment and curiosity without trying to control it in any way. Then, when our mind eventually wanders to something else like unhelpful ruminative thinking in the inner world or a sound in the outer world, we can gently and non-judgmentally return our attention to the breath. This formal practice may help to better regulate both focused and open attention so we are not stuck in problematic ruminative thinking, which can make our symptoms worse. Still, as a Christian trauma survivor, you may be wondering what a Christian perspective on all of this looks like. Let's look at what Scripture has to offer. Christians throughout the centuries have suggested that biblical meditation is a type of rumination, wherein we "chew on" scriptural truths as mantras to extract their nutrients for our psychological and spiritual benefit.[19]

A Christian Perspective

Within the New Testament of the Bible, the Apostle Paul instructed us to actively focus our attention on what is "true," "noble," "right," "lovely," "admirable," "excellent," and "praiseworthy."[20] So, what we intentionally choose to ruminate on within the Christian life is key, whether positive or negative.

One area of deeper ruminative, meditative focus for Christians can be God's promises found throughout the Old and New Testaments of the Bible. These promises of God can serve as the Christian equivalent to those found in LKM and the Buddhist tradition. They extend into the future and offer us needed hope from God in uncertain, ambiguous, and even seemingly dangerous seasons of life. Whereas trauma-based rumination may be compulsive and include the urge to unilaterally answer unanswerable "Why" and "What if" questions with an imperfect human mind, ruminating on God's promises can offer us confidence in a perfect God in a fallen, broken world.

The Puritans were Protestant Christians from England in the 1500s and 1600s who authentically attempted to apply an orthodox reading of the Bible to every area of life. They wrote quite a bit on God's promises. The Puritan scholar

J. I. Packer defined a promise as "a word that reaches into the future, creating a bond of obligation on the part of the one who gives it and of expectation on the part of the one who receives it."[21] With a promise, there are several ingredients. It includes a future obligation and relationship between two people as promisor and promisee. Writing centuries before Packer, the Puritan William Spurstowe suggested that God's promises capture "a declaration of God's will, in which he signifies what particular good things he will freely bestow, and the evils that he will remove."[22] And the Puritan Andrew Gray suggested that God's promises constitute "a glorious discovery of the good-will of God towards sinners... to bestow some spiritual or temporal good upon them..."[23] Here, we can see that God's promises consist of what he will carry out in the future based on his perfect will and omnibenevolence. Thus, it makes sense for Christians to ruminate and meditate on God's promises. This is because they are good for us mentally and spiritually, are trustworthy, and will be fulfilled based on what God has revealed in Scripture.

In the context of traumatic events, although we may continue to experience intrusive memories, distressing emotions, and compulsive ruminations, we can make the deliberate decision to shift toward ruminating and meditating on God's promises in the Bible. These promises may provide comfort amid the inevitability of suffering since we can effectively move from human uncertainty to divine certainty. We know how the story ends. The Bible has given us God's story of his relationship with humankind, discussed in detail in Chapter 3. This story begins with tragedy, separation, and trauma in the Garden of Eden, but it ends with unity and a "new heaven and a new earth."[24] We do not need to perseverate on human initiated "Why" and "What if" questions that may never lead to satisfying answers on this side of heaven. Rather, ruminating and meditating on God's promises, which extend well into the future, can help us with our trauma symptoms. Dwelling on God's promises can even protect us from the devastation of a completely shattered worldview,[25] given we are trusting that God is infinitely good and, therefore, will work things out for good.

But what are the types of promises that God has revealed in his Word, the Bible? And why might we need to ruminate and meditate on them as Christ followers? In 1619, the Puritan author Nicholas Byfield published an important work, *The Promises of God*, that attempted to answer these pressing questions for Christ followers. He began this salient writing with the following:

> The drift of this treatise is to show a godly Christian (who is already assured of God's favor, and knows he shall have abundant happiness when he dies and goes to heaven) how he may support his heart with sufficient contentment against all the miseries that can assault him from the time of his conversion, until his death.[26]

For Byfield, focusing on God's promises may very well have been the secret to contentment—an inner satisfaction in knowing that nothing is lacking in the here-and-now[27]—during instances of suffering. Many of God's promises offer us needed comfort in a fallen, broken world filled with no shortage of traumatic events. These promises are "places of Scripture which foretell what goodness the Lord will show to his people in affliction. For here belong all those promises which are given of purpose for the comforting and supporting of the godly in all their trials."[28] During the suffering that comes from trauma symptoms, we can turn to God for a deeper peace and well-being because he is infinitely good. Byfield further explained the benefits of sustained focus on God's promises:

> When a Christian first turns his thoughts towards the promises, the appearance of light and comfort which shine from them do oft-times seem to be as weak and imperfect rays which neither scatter fears nor darkness; [but] when again he sets himself to ripen and improve his thoughts upon them, then the evidence and comfort which they yield to the soul is both more clear and distinct; but when the heart and affections are fully fixed in the meditation of a promise, Oh! What a bright mirror is the promise then to the eye of faith![29]

When we devote our *full* attention with both head and heart to God's promises in Scripture, there may be tremendous psychological and spiritual benefits for Christians. This seems to be especially relevant for trauma survivors given the positive impact of focusing on such promises in place of unhelpful rumination. So much of our suffering involves being preoccupied with the past, where the traumatic event occurred. We also struggle to accept an uncertain and dangerous future, where we anticipate additional traumatic events occurring. God's promises are motivated by his infinite goodness and can help us fix our attention on the God of abounding love, not ruminate in isolation about the past or future. We can also shift from the many trauma-related questions we'll likely never get a sufficient answer to on this side of heaven since God is infinitely wise and we are not.

But what are these promises from God found in Scripture that can bring us comfort during trauma-related suffering? Within the Old and New Testaments,[30] we read of an abundance of promises:

- ❏ Exodus 34:6–7: "The Lord, the Lord, the compassionate and gracious God, slow to anger, abounding in love and faithfulness, maintaining love to thousands, and forgiving wickedness, rebellion and sin."
- ❏ Deuteronomy 31:6: "Never will I leave you; never will I forsake you."
- ❏ Psalm 91:14–16: "'Because he loves me,' says the Lord, 'I will rescue him; I will protect him, for he acknowledges my name. He will call

on me, and I will answer him; I will be with him in trouble, and I will deliver him and honor him. With long life I will satisfy him and show him my salvation.'"

❏ Psalm 145:13: "Your kingdom is an everlasting kingdom, and your dominion endures through all generations. The Lord is trustworthy in all he promises and faithful in all he does."

❏ Isaiah 43:1–2: "Do not fear, for I have redeemed you; I have summoned you by name; you are mine. When you pass through the waters, I will be with you. And when you pass through the rivers, they will not sweep over you. When you walk through the fire, you will not be burned; the flames will not set you ablaze. For I am the Lord your God, the Holy One of Israel, your Savior."

❏ Isaiah 43:5: "Do not be afraid, for I am with you."

❏ James 4:8: "Come near to God and he will come near to you."

❏ 1 Peter 5:7: "Cast all your anxiety on him because he cares for you."

Sprinkled across these passages, we read of God's obligatory love, care, grace, forgiveness, comfort, presence, protection, redemption, and trustworthiness. These promises of God are fixed and dependable, which can help trauma survivors to attain reassurance during moments of uncertainty and rumination. As we learn to shift our attention from trauma-based rumination to God's promises, I believe we are in a better position to manage our trauma symptoms such as intrusive memories, distressing emotions, and unhelpful perseverative thinking. But how can we practice this shift in a formal and biblically tethered manner? Drawing again from the Puritans, I believe we have an answer.

In the 1500s and 1600s, the Puritans wrote dozens of books on biblical meditation. They believed in the importance of anchoring themselves to Scripture to deeply ponder God's Word and apply it to every area of life. The Bible itself mentions meditation quite a bit. In the Old Testament, for instance, the Hebrew word *hagah* is used:

Blessed is the one who does not walk in step with the wicked or stand in the way that sinners take or sit in the company of mockers, but whose delight is in the law of the Lord, and who meditates on his law day and night. That person is like a tree planted by streams of water, which yields its fruit in season and whose leaf does not wither—whatever they do prospers.[31]

Building on this understanding that meditation is in fact biblical, the Puritan John Ball defined it as follows:

the steadfast and earnest bending of the mind on some spiritual and heavenly matter, discoursing on it with ourselves, until we bring it to some profitable point, both for the settling of our judgments, and the bettering of our hearts and lives.[32]

Here, we see that we are to "bend [or focus] the mind" on content that is "spiritual" and "heavenly." The need to bend here suggests there must be an intentional shift from that which is not beneficial to matters of a more spiritual or heavenly nature. We can use our God-given attention to shift our mental activity to what is good, which is God's special revelation—Scripture. We can use Scripture as a Christian mantra for our psychological and spiritual benefit. If mantras are simply statements deliberately repeated, we can ruminate on Christian scriptural mantras to positively impact our judgments and improve our inner and outer world.

Applied to trauma, we can shift our focus from trauma-based rumination to deeply reflecting, meditating, and ruminating on God's promises, which certainly qualify as spiritual truths.[33] For instance, holding on to God's promise that he will never leave us can help us when we struggle with trauma-based anxiety and unhelpful ruminative thoughts that the traumatic event will happen again. Upon doing so, we are keeping the mind occupied with the infinite goodness of God, which is extended into the future in the form of an unbreakable and trustworthy promise. When we regularly shift from unhelpful, earthly forms of rumination to heavenly, spiritual forms of rumination,[34] we are cultivating both focused and open forms of attention.

Returning to the writings of the Puritan William Spurstowe, we can meditate regularly on God's promises for optimal Christian functioning. As Spurstowe revealed, "One promise thoroughly ruminated and meditated on is likened to a morsel of meat well chewed and digested, which distributes more nourishment and strength to the body than great quantities taken down whole."[35] This meditative content that flows from God's Word, the Bible, can offer much-needed nourishment and strength for trauma survivors since we crave certainty in an uncertain world.

As mentioned in prior chapters, I recently researched with several colleagues the use of Christian meditation.[36] For one of the four weeks of the program, participants were instructed to meditate on God's promises in response to trauma-based rumination. Results revealed a decrease from before the four-week intervention began to after the intervention concluded in trauma-based rumination and trauma symptoms and an increase in the skill of attention. These findings suggest that distinctly Christian practices, not just Buddhist mindfulness meditation or LKM, may be helpful in reducing rumination and other symptoms. Such Christian practices may also increase attention on God and his Word as an important mental skill in the Christian life. Christians can learn to better regulate our attention using our own spiritual practices to ameliorate trauma-based mental suffering. Prior to practicing Christian attention, let's discuss an integrative perspective to consolidate what's been offered thus far.

An Integrative Perspective: Shifting from Trauma-Based Rumination to Ruminating on God's Promises[37]

To offer a more integrative viewpoint, after experiencing a traumatic event we may end up with unwanted and intrusive memories and distressing emotions. These memories may take the form of vivid details, images, or dreams of the event itself. Accompanying these memories, we may struggle with a range of emotions like fear, anxiety, guilt, shame, anger, and helplessness. To avoid these unwanted memories and emotions, we might engage in compulsive rumination. This type of perseveration is made up of asking abstract "Why" and "What if" questions about the event itself, the meaning of the event, or what the event means for the future.

Yet, when we stay stuck in this pattern of unhelpful rumination, we can exacerbate the very memories and emotions we are looking to avoid. Learning to pivot from counterproductive to productive rumination may be essential. If we are always ruminating and meditating on something, what we choose to meditate and ruminate on is key. We can cultivate attentional flexibility so we can better regulate what we focus on, which can play a sizeable role in how we respond to and manage trauma symptoms. For Christians, shifting our attention to positive rumination can consist of meditating on God's promises since they offer us needed hope, comfort, and confidence when we suffer from trauma symptoms. God's promises can also function as positive mantras for our psychological and spiritual benefit. We can repeat them throughout the day to remind us of who God is as infinitely good. Biblical meditation as a positive form of rumination with scriptural mantras can help us "chew on" and extract needed psychological and spiritual nutrients. This contrasts with relying on the "junk food" of unhelpful trauma-based rumination that doesn't improve our lives and, instead, may impair our functioning.

To make this salient shift, we need to develop a set of mental skills. Such skills start with Christian focused and open attention so we can ruminate in a sustained manner on God's promises in Scripture and be aware when we get stuck in unhelpful perseverative patterns. Essentially, we face a mental fork in the road each moment of life. Because our mind is always dwelling on, ruminating on, and meditating on cognitive material, we must decide which road to travel down—the helpful rumination road or the unhelpful rumination road. The skill of attention can help us make this shift from traveling down the unhelpful to helpful road. In turn, we can begin to get relief from the added suffering that comes from trauma symptoms. Let's now turn to the exercises in this chapter. We'll begin with a log to keep track of the types of rumination you might find yourself struggling with.

Exercises

Self-Monitoring Log

To begin the exercises in this chapter, please spend a day logging your experiences of intrusive memories, distressing emotions, unhelpful rumination, and coping efforts to shift your attention (see Table 5.1). This will give you a better sense of your current functioning. It will help you better understand when these trauma symptoms occur throughout the day, how you attempt to cope with them by shifting your attention, and your level of success in doing so as you continue with the chapter's activities. I've added an example in the 6:00 a.m. row to get you started. Please use extra paper if needed.

Once you have recorded your answers for a day, please respond to the below questions as best you can. Please use extra paper if needed.

1. What relationship, if any, emerged between your possible intrusive memories, distressing emotions, unhelpful ruminations, and coping strategies/level of success? Did you notice a certain pattern that materialized?

   _____

   _____

   _____

   _____

   _____

   _____

2. What types of rumination, if any, did you struggle with in response to possible intrusive memories and distressing emotions?

   _____

   _____

   _____

   _____

   _____

   _____

TABLE 5.1
Self-Monitoring Log

	Intrusive Memories/ Images/ Dreams	Distressing Emotions (Fear, Anxiety, Sadness, Anger, Guilt, Shame, Helplessness, Other)	Type of Unhelpful Rumination ("Why" Questions, "What If" Questions, Meaning of Event, Antecedents or Consequences of Event, Future Events)	Coping Strategy to Shift Attention (Thinking About Something Else/ Distraction, Hobby, Exercise, Television/ Smart Phone/Tablet, Relationship, Other)/ Level of Success
6:00 a.m.	*Image of prior car accident.*	*Intense fear and helplessness.*	*What if I get into another car accident that's worse?*	*Binge-watching Netflix to distract/not successful.*
7:00 a.m.				
8:00 a.m.				
9:00 a.m.				
10:00 a.m.				
11:00 a.m.				
12:00 p.m.				
1:00 p.m.				
2:00 p.m.				
3:00 p.m.				
4:00 p.m.				
5:00 p.m.				
6:00 p.m.				
7:00 p.m.				
8:00 p.m.				
9:00 p.m.				
10:00 p.m.				
11:00 p.m.				

3. How, if at all, did you attempt to shift your attention? Were you successful? Why or why not?

_____

_____

_____

_____

_____

_____

For this initial exercise, the goal is to begin to increase your self-awareness of the relationship between intrusive memories, distressing emotions, and unhelpful rumination. My hope is that you have also started to identify your various attempts to cope with the trauma symptoms and that some attentional strategies are more effective than others. This is in preparation for learning a new strategy. This strategy consists of meditating and ruminating on God's promises. Now that you are possibly more self-aware of the potential relationship between intrusive memories, distressing emotions, unhelpful rumination, and attentional coping strategies and your level of success, let's turn our attention to Christian meditation, a positive form of rumination. We will be practicing meditating on God's promises by utilizing Puritan meditation.

Developing Christian Attention by Meditating on God's Promises

With biblical meditation, first introduced in prior chapters, we can practice formally in solitude and silence or informally as we move about the day. The Puritans called formal practice deliberate meditation and informal practice occasional meditation.[38] To cultivate sustained attention, I'd like us to practice a formal version of meditation with the below steps. This type of deliberate meditation is a form of healthy rumination. It draws upon God's promises in Scripture to focus the mind on spiritual truths for our nourishment and comfort. With it, we use scriptural truths as Christian mantras for our psychological and spiritual benefit. You can also follow along with the audio file if you'd like: www.routledge.com/9781041088608.

To begin, find a quiet environment that is free from distractions. Sit up straight in a supportive chair with your eyes closed. Set aside at least 10 minutes for formal practice. Once you are ready, follow along with the below steps:[39]

1. Pray to God. Ask him to be with you for the next 10 minutes and help you shift from trauma-based rumination to his trustworthy and hope-filled scriptural promises.

2. Begin to repeat "Never will I leave you; never will I forsake you" from Deuteronomy 31:6 with focused and sustained attention. Do so slowly, gently, and within your mind.

3. When your mind inevitably drifts to something other than the "Never will I leave you" verse such as intrusive memories, distressing emotions, or trauma-based rumination, simply return your attention to the verse. Do so with non-judgment and open attention. No matter how many times your mind drifts, just bring it back with an attitude of grace.

4. As you continue to recite the verse slowly, gently, and within, deeply feel God's presence. He is with you right now and will not abandon you.

5. As this meditative practice ends, commit to ruminating on this verse throughout the day as you move from deliberate to occasional meditation.

6. Pray again to God. Thank him for his promise to be with you and never abandon you.

After concluding the practice, try to journal for a few minutes about your experience with the below questions (please use extra paper if needed):

1. What was it like to spend this time with God?

_____

_____

_____

_____

_____

_____

2. How well were you able to focus your attention on God's promises?

_____

_____

_____

_____

_____

_____

3. What was it like to shift your attention back to God's promises when your mind inevitably drifted?

_____

_____

_____

_____

_____

_____

4. How well did meditating on God's promises help you shift from intrusive memories, distressing emotions, and/or trauma-based rumination if these experiences emerged?

_____

_____

_____

_____

_____

_____

5. How can you make room for this practice in daily life in a deliberate manner? How can you move from deliberate to occasional meditation throughout the day by informally meditating and ruminating on God's promises when you get distracted with intrusive memories, distressing emotions, or trauma-based rumination?

_____

_____

_____

_____

_____

_____

You can select other verses that capture God's promises such as those mentioned previously in the chapter to also meditate on. In either case, my suggestion is to select *short* passages in Scripture so that you can savor them and easily memorize and meditate and ruminate on them. This is reminiscent of taking a small, not large, bite out of food. Before we conclude the chapter, I'd like to present a real-world example of Christian attention in action for a trauma survivor.

Case Example

Eric grew up in a Protestant Christian home in a middle-class neighborhood. His parents took him to church just about every Sunday. At church, he learned that God is in control of this world. For Eric, God's infinite power combined with God's infinite love and wisdom meant that God wanted what was best for Eric. God also knew all possible scenarios for Eric and was able to carry out the best plan for Eric. With this understanding of God, Eric developed a deep trust in the Trinitarian God of the Bible.

Yet, when Eric was a teenager, he came home from school one afternoon to find a masked gunman robbing his family home. With Eric's parents still at work, he walked through the front door and was met with a gun in his face. "Freeze," the intruder violently yelled as he quickly aimed the gun point-blank at Eric. For what seemed like an eternity, Eric was frozen in place and overwhelmed with fear. His mind raced with thoughts of dying. In this moment, Eric truly believed at his core that he had just taken his last breath.

Eric chose to run. In a panic, he turned his back on the intruder and fled. With his back exposed, he anticipated getting shot as he raced to the door. However, he heard no gun go off and felt no bullets piercing his skin. Once outside, Eric ran up the street to a neighbor's home to call the police. Thankfully, the police responded to the call. They quickly surrounded the house and eventually detained the intruder in a nearby residence.

Although Eric was no longer in immediate danger and later testified in court to help convict the intruder, he continued to have vivid memories and dreams of the gun being pointed at him. These intrusive images left Eric feeling overwhelmed with fear and anxiety. As he struggled to manage these emotions, he often ruminated. "Why, God, did you let this happen to me?" he would frequently ask. "What if it happens again, God?" he would perseverate on. Despite the persistence of these unending questions, he never really came up with satisfying answers to bring him peace and comfort. Instead, he came to realize he was becoming more and more preoccupied and distracted. To make matters worse, these ongoing ruminations often increased the frequency of Eric's memories of the event and feelings of fear and anxiety. Eric longed for the days of his childlike faith, wherein he trusted in God's infinite goodness, wisdom, and power to protect him and keep him safe in a fallen world.

Without intervention, Eric would continue to struggle with feeling safe in his family home for the next several years. Similar sounds, such as the house settling, had the capacity to create those same feelings of fear as Eric imagined the noise to be the telltale sign of an intruder. His life, especially at night in the supposed comfort of his own home, was unbearable as his mind methodically reviewed the various ways in which the intruder might return to finish the job. Many nights, he would cry out to God by asking "Why can't I just get over this and feel safe again?"

On one Sunday morning, his pastor gave a sermon on the importance of meditating on God's promises in the Christian life. This intrigued Eric. Could Eric begin to trust in the promises that God made in the Bible when he started to ruminate? Might he set aside dedicated time to meditate on such promises as an antidote to an overactive, doubting, and fearful mind?

Isaiah 43:5 was especially impactful for Eric: "Do not be afraid, for I am with you." As he began to recite this verse to himself both in the quiet of his home and throughout the day, he noticed that his mind was less distracted with unhelpful rumination. Although by no means a perfect remedy, he realized he was able to pivot to this verse when he started to perseverate on the wrong things. For Eric, deeply pondering, meditating on, ruminating on, and focusing on God's promises slowly rebuilt his trust in God's infinite goodness, wisdom, and power. He also could fill his mind with hope in God's perfect will and not his own understanding. Slowly, he was able to develop both open and focused attention to dually notice when he began to ruminate in unhelpful ways and shift toward ruminating on the scriptural promises of God.

Conclusion

Because traumatic events are so powerful and sometimes life threatening, they can bring with them a variety of intrusive memories and distressing emotions. In response, we may begin to ruminate in unhelpful ways. This rumination might take on a life of its own because we often struggle to manage it. We may even have more distressing memories and emotions that leave us stuck. Learning to shift from unhelpful to helpful types of rumination with the mental skill of attention may be especially effective. To do so, meditative practices can be useful. Meditation may allow us to develop both focused and open attention as we regularly shift from unhelpful to helpful rumination. We can notice with greater distance and flexibility when we are stuck in problematic ruminative patterns.

For Christians, God has promised us many future outcomes in the Bible. These can bring us comfort and hope because he is infinitely good and will carry them out. When deciding what to focus and ruminate on, God's promises may be especially relevant for trauma survivors since they include themes of safety, protection, and love. As Christians living in a fallen world, although we may not be able to avoid the traumatic events that occur, we can learn to shift our attention to God when earthly preoccupations become overwhelming, distracting, and impairing. My prayer is that this chapter has helped you consider alternative ways to manage trauma-related intrusive memories and distressing emotions as you turn from fallible human rumination to ruminating on the God who is infallible and good. In the next chapter, we discuss the role that Christian focus on the present moment can play in shifting from unhelpful, earthly to helpful, spiritual rumination as we recognize God's omnipresence from moment to moment.

Notes

1 APA Dictionary (n.d.b).
2 Lutz et al. (2008).
3 Lutz et al. (2008).
4 This paragraph is based on a review of Birrer and Michael (2011), Ehlers and Clark (2000), Michael et al. (2007), and Moulds et al. (2020).
5 Ehlers and Clark (2000).
6 Merriam-Webster (n.d.).
7 Vest (2008).
8 Keator (2018).
9 Cann et al. (2011); Michael et al. (2007); Ramos et al. (2018).
10 Cann et al. (2011).
11 Cann et al. (2011).
12 García et al. (2017).
13 García et al. (2017).
14 Michael et al. (2007).
15 Im and Follette (2016).
16 Hawley et al. (2014).
17 Wang et al. (2021).
18 Throughout the chapter, I use "mantra" to simply mean the slow, intentional repetition of statements to focus the mind on positive cognitive material. In Christianity, mantras can be the name of God, scriptural phrases, or prayer words. Within the Christian tradition, mantras have been used to focus the mind and are embedded in meditative and prayer practices. This contrasts with mantras in Buddhism and Hinduism that function as sacred or mystical utterances that emphasize sounds for the purpose of relaxation. In secular psychology, mantras have been used in recent years as interventions for psychological benefits (Oman, 2024).
19 Keator (2018).
20 Philippians 4:8.

21 Packer (2009).
22 Spurstowe (2012).
23 Quoted in Beeke and La Belle (2010).
24 See Genesis 3 and Revelation 21.
25 Janoff-Bulman (1992).
26 Byfield (2013).
27 Knabb et al. (2021).
28 Byfield (2013).
29 Byfield (2013).
30 See also Beeke and La Belle (2010).
31 Psalm 1:1–3.
32 Ball (2016).
33 Holman Bible Dictionary (2004a).
34 Colossians 3:2.
35 Spurstowe (2012).
36 Knabb et al. (2022).
37 This section is based on a review of Ball (2016); Byfield (2013); Cann et al. (2011); Knabb et al. (2019a, 2019c, 2022); Michael et al. (2007); and Moulds et al. (2020).
38 Beeke and Jones (2012).
39 This six-step meditation is based on Ball (2016), Beeke and Jones (2012), and Knabb (2021), with portions from Knabb et al. (2019c).

CHAPTER 6

Skill 2

Christian Focus on the Present Moment

Introduction

In the second skill-based chapter, we'll discuss Christian focus on the present moment. First, we'll explore a secular psychological perspective on the role that the present moment plays in trauma symptoms and trauma-based rumination. Then, we'll review a Christian perspective on practicing the presence of God, which can help you pivot from unhelpful rumination to a real relationship with the Triune God of the Bible. In the process, we'll unpack definitions, examples, and exercises to assist you in making this salient shift throughout the day. With this shift, you'll hopefully begin to see God's presence in all of life. To conclude, I'll share a real-life story to demonstrate how to apply this skill, Christian focus on the present moment, to trauma-based psychological suffering.

A Secular Psychological Perspective

Within secular psychology, authors sometimes refer to a problematic state of mind called "automatic pilot."[1] With automatic pilot, we are constantly distracted from the present moment. Like automatic pilot technology on an airplane, the pilot isn't flying the plane and doesn't need to control the plane in any way. For humans, automatic pilot means we aren't really thinking about or experiencing what we are doing in front of us. We aren't being intentional

DOI: 10.4324/9781003647270-6

and purposeful. We are distracted. These distractions often come from inner cognitive experiences like overthinking with rumination. When we are on automatic pilot, we are unaware of the person we are talking to or the activity we are engaged in within the outer world. We are thinking about the past or future and lost within the inner world. We are preoccupied with thoughts and, as a result, unaware of what is unfolding in the environment.

For example, on a Wednesday evening, I may drive home from work and pull into my driveway. As I get out of my car to go into my house, I may be unaware of the sensory experience I just had of driving home. I may have forgotten the route I just drove. This is because I was ruminating about the day by going over and over a conversation I had with a coworker ("What if I said something stupid?" "What if she now hates me?" "What if I ruined my reputation?"). Since I was distracted by my ruminative mind, I was unable to focus on the sensory experience of driving home in the real world (e.g., seeing the cars around me, smelling the air freshener in my car, hearing honking horns in the distance, feeling my hands on the leather steering wheel). This sensory experience is what keeps me anchored to the present moment and engaged with the world around me. In life, we need to balance the thinking mind and the inner world with sensory experiences and the outer world.

Tragically, most of life can be lived on automatic pilot. We may end up lost and distracted because we have not developed the skill of intentionally focusing on the present moment. We miss out on living life to the fullest. Automatic pilot can become so habitual that we don't even realize we are missing the events that are unfolding before us. We may be distracted from watching our child's baseball game, worshipping God during Sunday morning church service, getting important directions from a boss or coworker about how to complete a needed task, or having a conversation about the day with a friend or family member.

Because of how vulnerable we can be to slipping into automatic pilot mode, we need a regular strategy for shifting to full connection with the here-and-now. Although we may be lost in the mind dozens of times per day, each time we notice we are on automatic pilot is an opportunity to return our focus to the present moment. All hope is not lost. Automatic pilot is sort of like our default mode of the mind as human beings. We need to be intentional about bringing our attention and focus back to the present moment.

When it comes to automatic pilot and trauma-based rumination, we may experience initial intrusive memories about a past traumatic event. In response, we may end up ruminating about these vivid, lifelike memories. From there, automatic pilot may kick in without us even realizing it. As we go about our day, we may be unaware of conversations or activities in the outer world because we are so distracted within the inner world with trauma-based rumination. Unfortunately, this may mean that we are suffering and distracted from living life to the fullest. Not only is trauma-based rumination unhelpful, but it can also lead to the experience of missing out on savoring and enjoying life.

Remember that trauma-based rumination can be a mental avoidance strategy.[2] We may ruminate about the traumatic event to cognitively avoid the difficult intrusive memory and accompanying distressing emotion. When we ask "Why" ("Why did this happen to me?") and "What if" ("What if it happens again?") questions about the causes and consequences of the event, we may not actually process what's needed.[3] It prevents us from trying to accurately make sense of and truly process what happened and how we felt (and currently feel) about it.[4] Ultimately, rumination may not work and can keep us stuck on automatic pilot. Not only may it increase the very memories and emotions we are trying to avoid,[5] it can also distract us from life. It is an ineffective coping strategy.

Thankfully, secular psychologists have developed strategies for shifting from automatic pilot to a greater awareness of the present moment. When we can focus on the present moment, rather than getting distracted by intrusive memories, distressing emotions, and rumination, we can more fully engage with the world around us. And this authentic engagement with the world can enrich life so that each moment is intentional and meaningful.

One such strategy to help with trauma symptoms is mindfulness meditation, introduced in prior chapters.[6] This type of meditation developed several millennia ago in the Buddhist religious tradition. It has been succinctly defined as "non-attached awareness."[7] With this meditative strategy, we are attempting to approach each unfolding moment with purposeful attention.[8] We are also relating to each moment with non-judgment.[9] Each moment is new, different, and novel. Instead of allowing our mind to judge each moment as somehow not quite right or needing to be changed, we are accepting whatever is before us with openness and curiosity.

As one of many skills developed within mindfulness meditation, focusing on the present moment can offer the needed antidote to the psychological suffering that comes from traumatic events. So much of our trauma-related suffering results from mentally living in the past or future. It's as if we are time traveling with our mind to the past and future throughout the day.[10] This mental time traveling prevents us from living life to the fullest in each unfolding moment.

With the past, we have the intrusive, unwanted memory itself, which may come in the form of a vivid dream, flashback, or image. Although the memory certainly seems real, it only exists in our mind. This is because the traumatic event is in the past and long gone. Yet, we convince ourselves that we are re-experiencing the traumatic event in the present because it seems so real and lifelike. In turn, we may struggle with a range of distressing emotions, like fear, anxiety, guilt, shame, or anger. We may experience guilt because we believe we could have done something to avoid the event in the past or anxiety because we anticipate the event happening again. Looking out into the future, we may predict with confidence that we will be traumatized all over again. However, the anticipation of future traumatic events also takes place in the mind.

With mindfulness meditation, we have a gateway to the present moment.[11] With this ability to focus on the here-and-now, we can be more fully engaged, alive, and alert to what is unfolding before us in the outer world, not pre-occupied with the inner world. As we learn to keep our attention on what is before us in each unfolding moment, we are less likely to get stuck in patterns of unhelpful rumination that make intrusive memories and distressing emotions worse.

As a quick example, with mindfulness of breathing, we are focusing on each breath in the here-and-now with an attitude of open curiosity and non-judgment. We may focus on the breath going in and out of our mouth or lungs or our abdomen expanding and constricting. Whenever a distracting experience in the inner world (like a thought, feeling, sensation, memory, or image) or outer world (such as a sound in the distance) pulls us away from focusing on our breathing, we simply return our wandering attention to the breath.

Or we may be mindful as we are eating a meal. With this practice, we can use the five senses to experience each bite like it is taking place for the first time. We may focus on the texture of the food as we chew, followed by the taste, then the smell. As we fully engage with each bite, we are more present to the experience. We can savor and enjoy each bite because we are present to the simple event of eating. This is contrasted with being on automatic pilot while eating food, unaware we just consumed a meal and, consequently, unable to enjoy the experience in the here-and-now.

We may practice these simple mindfulness-based activities for 10 or 20 minutes. The benefits include learning to focus on simple experiences in the present moment with an open curiosity and bringing our focus back when it has drifted to a thought about the past or future. Over time, using our senses to engage with the outer world can help us stay rooted in the here-and-now since we are always interacting with our environment. In the process, we are learning to experience seemingly boring or mundane activities (like following the breath or chewing a bite of food) as exciting and new. This brings everything to life in interesting and vibrant ways.

Research has revealed that mindfulness meditation may be helpful in reducing trauma symptoms. For example, in a review of close to 20 studies on mindfulness-based interventions for symptoms of posttraumatic stress, results revealed that the regular practice of mindfulness as a form of meditation was helpful in reducing such symptoms.[12] The authors of this review pointed out that mindfulness-based meditative practices may be helpful because they allow practitioners with a history of trauma to focus on the present moment, not the past or future, with an attitude of non-judgment. Mindfulness meditation can help those who regularly practice stay anchored to the here-and-now with an open, curious, non-judgmental attitude toward whatever comes up in the inner world and a greater sensory awareness of the outer world. This is in contrast with ruminating as a form of avoidance, fixating on the past traumatic event, and getting stuck on automatic pilot.

For Christians, we have our own religious tradition to turn to, not Buddhism and mindfulness. Rather than being alone in the present moment to practice mindfulness as an individualized form of meditation, Christians believe in a personal, loving God. Let's now shift to a Christian understanding of the present moment, where God is with us and actively responding to our needs, including our trauma-based suffering.

A Christian Perspective

From a Christian perspective, the Bible, spanning Genesis to Revelation, reveals the story of God's pursuit of humankind, first introduced in prior chapters.[13] In Genesis, we read that God created humankind to be in relationship with him. Yet, we also learn in Genesis that the fall of humankind led to humankind's separation from God. Because Adam and Eve wanted to be like God, not dependent on him, they were banished from the Garden of Eden. Fast-forward to the New Testament, and we read about God's deliberate plan to restore humankind's relationship with him. By sending God's Son to die on a cross to pay the price for the sins of the world, those who believe in Jesus have a personal relationship with God again and will be with him forever.

This story of relationship also reveals that God deeply cares for his creation and wants to be involved in our individual lives. Instead of being distant and apathetic, the God of the Bible is a God of loving presence. The Bible captures who God is through what are called his attributes (already mentioned in some detail in Chapter 3). These are qualities of God, such as God's infinite love and presence. For example, we read in Psalm 139:7–10,

> Where can I go from your Spirit? Where can I flee from your presence? If I go up to the heavens, you are there; if I make my bed in the depths, you are there. If I rise on the wings of the dawn, if I settle on the far side of the sea, even there your hand will guide me, your right hand will hold me fast.

As another example, in 1 John 4:16 we learn that "God is love." Finally, possibly the most famous verse in the Bible, John 3:16 reveals that "God so loved the world that he gave his one and only Son, that whoever believes in him shall not perish but have eternal life." These attributes suggest that God loves us, is always with us, and wants to give us an abundant life with him. God's character is highly relevant for this chapter on the importance of the present moment when responding to trauma symptoms.

After a traumatic event, Christian trauma survivors may get stuck ruminating about the event itself. We may ask unanswerable questions in a perseverative manner, such as "Why did this happen to me, God?" or "Where were you when this happened, God?" or "Will you protect me so that this doesn't happen again, God?" Crying out to God amid our pain certainly makes sense, since God hears our cries.[14] Still, repeatedly asking these questions may be a way to avoid the intrusive memories and distressing emotions that can come from traumatic events. With such endless rumination, we can get stuck on automatic pilot, which distracts us from life. Rumination can end up increasing, not decreasing, the frequency of our intrusive thoughts and distressing emotions[15] and getting in the way of enjoying life in the here-and-now.

So, in this chapter I'd like to propose an alternative to trauma-based rumination—practicing God's presence. Like focusing on the present moment with mindfulness meditation, as a Christian trauma survivor you can learn an intentional strategy to shift from the past or future to the immediacy of the here-and-now. Yet, unlike mindfulness meditation, practicing God's presence is a relational approach. Because the God of the Bible is infinitely loving and present, he is with you right here and now. His love is endless, and his presence is everywhere. He hears your cries and is responsive to your needs in each passing second of the day.

With this understanding in mind, as Christians we need a simple strategy to recognize that God is with us in each unfolding moment. We can learn to acknowledge his loving presence in all of life, not just on Sunday mornings at church. We can recognize his loving companionship while we are taking out the trash or vacuuming the house. We can spend time with him while driving to work or paying the bills. We can even practice God's presence when we are suffering from trauma symptoms.

Practicing God's presence is like enjoying a conversation with a close friend in your car as the two of you drive on a cross-country trip to see the vast United States. Although there are certainly a range of distractions on the road, like stoplights, honking cars, potholes, and wildlife running across the road, you can remain focused on the presence of and conversation with your friend as you enjoy life together. You can deliberately choose to cherish each unfolding moment, no matter what distractions arise.

Likewise, focusing on God's presence is like traveling with *him* on the roads of life, no matter where the road takes you or what distractions you encounter. With God, you always have a traveling companion to enjoy life with. Practicing the presence of God can help you recognize that he is active and present in both your inner and outer world. He is loving you and ministering to your needs. Remaining aware of this can help you shift from trauma-based rumination to God throughout the day, not remain stuck on automatic pilot. One such strategy comes from a humble French monk from several centuries ago.

Brother Lawrence was a French monk who lived a simple life in the 1600s. He apparently washed dishes and made sandals to occupy the time. During his humble days, others increasingly sought him out for spiritual advice because of his reputation for practicing God's presence in even the most basic activities.[16] These experiences were documented in the now famous book, *The Practice of the Presence of God.* In this book, simple guidelines are offered to help Christians recognize God's active, loving presence in all of life, whether washing dishes, making sandals, eating a meal, gardening, or engaging in other regular tasks. By "slowly," "carefully," "deliberately," "gently," and "lovingly" completing such daily activities, we can acknowledge God in the here-and-now.[17] We can relate to him as a close friend as we carry out each day's requirements.[18] To capture this simple psychological and spiritual skill, Brother Lawrence offered the following:

> The holiest, most ordinary, and most necessary practice of the spiritual life is that of the presence of God. It is to take delight in and become accustomed to his divine company, speaking humbly and conversing lovingly with him all the time, at every moment, without rule or measure, especially in times of temptation, suffering, or weariness.[19]

Brother Lawrence taught that we must do the following to practice God's presence in each unfolding moment of the day:

> We must continually apply ourselves so that all our actions, without exception, become a kind of brief conversation with God, not in a contrived manner but coming from the purity and simplicity of our hearts.[20]

He also said,

> We must perform all our actions carefully and deliberately, not impulsively or hurriedly, for such would characterize a distracted mind. We must work gently and lovingly with God, asking him to accept our work.[21]

According to Brother Lawrence, focusing on God in the present moment is about applying "our mind to God, or a remembrance of God present" by "[formulating] a few words interiorly, such as: 'My God, I am completely yours.'"[22]

In this chapter, you will focus on God's presence as you complete a simple daily activity. As you complete the activity, you will also repeat to yourself within "My God, I am completely yours." This pairing of a simple activity and phrase will help you shift from trauma-based rumination to God's loving presence in the immediacy of each moment, rather than being on automatic pilot.[23]

As a reminder, a few years ago several colleagues and I researched the use of Christian meditative practices for trauma symptoms.[24] In the second week of the four-week program, we asked the Christian study participants to practice God's presence. This was done to shift from trauma-based rumination and automatic pilot to God's loving presence in the here-and-now. We wanted them to shift from being preoccupied with the inner world to being more engaged with the outer world. They were to intentionally recognize God's active, loving presence in their environment. After four weeks, the Christian participants reported a decrease in trauma-based rumination and trauma symptoms and an increase in their ability to focus on the present moment. So, instead of Buddhist mindfulness, Christians can learn to attend to God in the present moment for psychological healing. Before moving on to the exercises in this chapter, I'd like to consolidate what we have covered thus far.

An Integrative Perspective: Shifting from Trauma-Based Rumination to Practicing God's Presence

To offer an integrative understanding, as a trauma survivor you may struggle with intrusive, unwanted memories about the traumatic event like flashbacks, dreams, or images. You may also experience distressing emotions that accompany the memories, such as fear, anxiety, anger, or shame. To try to distance yourself from the unwelcome memories and emotions, you may begin to ruminate by asking "Why" ("Why did this happen to me, God?") and "What if" ("What if it happens again, God?") questions. This type of rumination can lead to automatic pilot being your default mode of the mind. Although rumination as a cognitive coping strategy seems to make sense, given thinking about the event may prevent you from having to relive the memories and feel the extremely difficult emotions, it may make the memories and emotions worse. It may also distract you from fully showing up to and savoring each unfolding moment of life.

So, if rumination on automatic pilot doesn't work, what might be an alternative? Last chapter, we focused on the skill of attention to shift from trauma-based rumination to God's promises. This chapter, we will be emphasizing

God's presence in the here-and-now. The reason practicing God's presence may be helpful, both psychologically and spiritually, is because we are learning to successfully pivot. We are shifting from perseverative, unanswerable "Why" and "What if" questions that keep us preoccupied with the past or future to God's loving presence in the now. Like a trustworthy traveling companion on a cross-country road trip, we can enjoy the landscapes of life in each unfolding moment. We can do so even if we end up encountering potholes, bad weather, roadkill, or car trouble.

Exercises

Self-Monitoring Log

To begin the exercises in this chapter, please spend a day logging your experiences of intrusive memories, distressing emotions, unhelpful rumination, and coping efforts to focus on the present moment (see Table 6.1). This will give you a better sense of your current functioning. It will help you better understand when these trauma symptoms occur throughout the day, how you attempt to cope with them by focusing on the present moment, and your level of success in doing so as you continue with the chapter's activities. I've added an example in the 6:00 a.m. row to get you started. Please use extra paper if needed.

Once you have recorded your answers for a day, please respond to the below questions as best you can. Please use extra paper if needed.

1. What relationship, if any, emerged between your possible intrusive memories, distressing emotions, unhelpful ruminations, and coping strategies/level of success? Did you notice a certain pattern that materialized?

    _____

    _____

    _____

    _____

    _____

    _____

TABLE 6.1
Self-Monitoring Log

	Intrusive Memories/ Images/ Dreams	Distressing Emotions (Fear, Anxiety, Sadness, Anger, Guilt, Shame, Helplessness, Other)	Type of Unhelpful Rumination ("Why" Questions, "What If" Questions, Meaning of Event, Antecedents or Consequences of Event, Future Events)	Coping Strategy to Focus on Present Moment (Hobby, Exercise, Television/Smart Phone/Tablet, Relationship, Other)/Level of Success
6:00 a.m.	*Image of past abuse.*	*Intense fear and shame.*	*What if I am abused again?*	*Playing video games to focus on the present moment/not successful.*
7:00 a.m.				
8:00 a.m.				
9:00 a.m.				
10:00 a.m.				
11:00 a.m.				
12:00 p.m.				
1:00 p.m.				
2:00 p.m.				
3:00 p.m.				
4:00 p.m.				
5:00 p.m.				
6:00 p.m.				
7:00 p.m.				
8:00 p.m.				
9:00 p.m.				
10:00 p.m.				
11:00 p.m.				

2. What types of rumination, if any, did you struggle with in response to possible intrusive memories and distressing emotions?

_____

_____

_____

_____

_____

_____

3. How, if at all, did you attempt to focus on the present moment? Were you successful? Why or why not?

_____

_____

_____

_____

_____

_____

Like the last chapter, the goal is to begin to increase your self-awareness of the relationship between intrusive memories, distressing emotions, rumination, and coping strategies (this time by focusing on the present moment). This newfound awareness can help you prepare for a different, more intentional strategy—practicing the presence of God. Let's turn now to a spiritual exercise offered by Brother Lawrence to focus on the present moment, where God is ministering to you each unfolding second of the day.

Practicing Christian Focus on the Present Moment[25]

To practice God's presence, first introduced in prior chapters, you will be engaging in the simple activity of walking. You will pair walking in your neighborhood with recognizing God's presence in the here-and-now. Try to set a specific time each day to walk, find a quiet environment to walk that is free from major distractions, silence or turn off your smart phone, and walk at a slow pace for the full 10 minutes as you follow the below instructions. You can also follow along with the audio file if you'd like: www.routledge.com/978104 1088608.

1. "Slowly," "carefully," "deliberately," "gently," and "lovingly" complete the designated activity (in this case, walking).
2. As you complete the activity, "interiorly" say to yourself "My God, I am completely yours."
3. When your mind inevitably wanders to a distraction in the inner world like trauma-based rumination or the outer world like a noisy car driving by, gently and lovingly return your focus to the pairing of the activity (walking) and phrase ("My God, I am completely yours").

Upon conclusion of the 10-minute practice, try to journal for a few minutes about your experience with the below questions (please use extra paper if needed):

1. What was it like to spend this time with God in the here-and-now?

_____

_____

_____

_____

_____

_____

2. How well were you able to focus on God in the present moment as you engaged in the activity of walking?

_____

_____

_____

_____

_____

_____

3. What was it like to refocus yourself on the activity and phrase when you inevitably drifted to something else (whether internally or externally)?

_____

_____

_____

_____

_____

_____

4. How well did practicing God's presence help you shift from intrusive memories, distressing emotions, and/or trauma-based rumination if these experiences emerged?

_____

_____

_____

_____

_____

_____

5. How can you set aside time for this practice in daily life? How can you practice God's presence throughout the day when you get distracted with intrusive memories, distressing emotions, or trauma-based rumination?

_____

_____

_____

_____

_____

_____

Remember that you can practice God's presence by pairing *any* simple activity with a short phrase to acknowledge him in the here-and-now. You might practice God's presence when washing the dishes, folding clothes, mowing the lawn, or driving your car. No matter what seemingly boring or mundane activity you are completing, you can always remember God in the immediacy of the moment. You can focus your attention on him, not the trauma-based rumination and automatic pilot that can keep you stuck and distracted in life. Let's now turn to a case example to see practicing God's presence in action, prior to concluding the chapter.

Case Example

Emma didn't grow up in a Christian home. Her father was Jewish, and her mother was agnostic. In college, though, she dated a Christian man, Ray, who introduced her to other Christian friends. During this time, she started attending a local Protestant church. There, she first learned that the God of the Bible is a God of loving presence.

One Sunday morning sermon, she began to feel overwhelmed with a sense that God was present with her in the church building. She experienced God as with her and loving her in the immediacy of the moment. For the first time, she felt like God knew her and cared for her.

After college, she married Ray, and the two of them quickly started to plan for a family. Roughly a year later, she was pregnant. During the first few months of her pregnancy, she felt God's loving presence. As she talked with Ray about baby names, her realization that she would be a mother only grew.

Yet, on one tragic evening about half-way through her pregnancy, she started showing signs of a miscarriage. Panicked and afraid, Ray and Emma quickly drove to a local hospital for treatment. After a series of tests, the young couple learned that they had lost the baby, who they had already named Luke. Devastated, they didn't know what to do. They held each other and sobbed, struggling to make sense of what had just happened.

Shortly after this traumatic event, Emma started to have vivid nightmares of the miscarriage. During the day, she also struggled with intrusive images of where she was at in her house when the miscarriage started, the car ride to the hospital, and the hospital room itself when she learned the overwhelming news. With these images came overwhelming emotions. She felt fear and anxiety because she doubted if she could have a baby again. She also struggled with a sense of guilt. She wondered if she somehow caused the miscarriage even though there was no evidence to suggest it was her fault.

In response to these vivid nightmares and images and the accompanying emotional distress, she started to ruminate to try to distance herself from the difficult memories and feelings. She would get stuck asking "Why" and "What if" questions repeatedly: "Why, God, did you allow this to happen?" "Why didn't I get to see my baby?" and "What if I can't have children, God?" Unfortunately, these questions did not lead to satisfying answers or a needed resolution. Instead, she was distracted and miserable. And the questions only seemed to agitate her more. The more questions she asked in a repetitive way, the more the memories and emotions came flooding in. After weeks of suffering, her husband encouraged her to make an appointment to see a local Christian counselor.

In their first counseling session, the professional counselor, Dr. Evans, helped Emma to better understand that she had experienced a traumatic event. Following the event, she was struggling with trauma symptoms, including intrusive memories, distressing emotions, and trauma-based rumination. Over the next several weeks, Dr. Evans learned more about Emma's religious background and current relationship with God. Because she was a Christian, he assisted her in beginning to practice God's presence to get unstuck from the unhelpful types of rumination that intensified her trauma-based memories and emotions. This was especially important because her rumination had led to automatic pilot being her default mode of mind. She was unable to be present in her marriage or church life.

During one especially powerful session about a month into treatment, Emma recalled her earlier experiences of God's loving presence. Building on this fond memory, Dr. Evans helped her to notice when she began to ruminate, then practice God's presence by slowly and gently repeating "My God, I am completely yours." Gradually, she was able to practice God's presence throughout the day. She was able to successfully pivot from unanswerable "Why" and "What if" questions. This experience of God's love in the immediacy of the moment allowed her to take her perseverative mind off the past so she could find loving comfort from God in each unfolding moment.

Emma continued to work with Dr. Evans for several months to process the traumatic event more fully. She continued to struggle with some trauma-related symptoms. Yet, this compact practice of focusing on the God of love in the here-and-now by pairing simple daily activities with a short phrase helped her. She was able to dually deepen her relationship with God and get unstuck from unhelpful forms of rumination and automatic pilot.

Conclusion

Traumatic events and corresponding intrusive memories and distressing emotions can leave us preoccupied with the past or future. In response, we need a simple strategy for anchoring ourselves to the present moment. Although rumination seems to provide some distance from difficult memories and emotions, it may lead to automatic pilot. This common mode of the mind, being lost in our head, can rob us of the enjoyment of life's unfolding moments. Deliberate efforts are needed to pivot from the unhelpful rumination that dwells on the past to the here-and-now.

Although mindfulness meditation can be a helpful intervention for trauma symptoms, Christians may prefer to turn to our own religious heritage for relief. Brother Lawrence's teachings on practicing God's presence may be a fitting alternative. This Christian alternative is also supported by my own original research, reviewed above, which has revealed that such practices can help to reduce trauma symptoms, including trauma-based rumination.

By pairing simple daily activities with a short phrase that acknowledges God's presence in the here-and-now, Christian trauma survivors can learn to pivot from automatic pilot, with its accompanying rumination, to the God of love. This God of love is with us as a trustworthy traveling companion, regardless of the distractions of life. We can learn to practice his presence and get unstuck from unhelpful perseverations that only intensify the symptoms we are trying to avoid. Building on the first two skill-based chapters, next, we explore Christian awareness as an intentional strategy for relating to trauma symptoms with greater compassion.

Notes

1 Crane (2009).
2 Bishop et al. (2018); Michael et al. (2007); Ramos et al. (2018).
3 Ehlers and Clark (2000).
4 Ehlers and Clark (2000).
5 Michael et al. (2007).
6 Follette et al. (2006).
7 Germer (2009).
8 Bishop et al. (2004).
9 Bishop et al. (2004).
10 Hayes et al. (2012).
11 Bishop et al. (2004).
12 Hopwood and Schutte (2017).
13 This paragraph is based on a review of Wright (2006).
14 Psalm 18:6.
15 Michael et al. (2007).
16 Lawrence (2015).
17 Lawrence (2015).
18 Lawrence (2015).
19 Lawrence (2015).

20 Lawrence (2015).
21 Lawrence (2015).
22 Lawrence (2015).
23 Segal et al. (2012).
24 Knabb et al. (2022).
25 This exercise is based on the teachings of Lawrence (2015), with portions from Knabb et al. (2019c).

CHAPTER 7

Skill 3

Christian Awareness

Introduction

In the third skill-based chapter, we'll explore Christian awareness. We'll begin by discussing a secular psychological perspective on the role that compassionate, kind awareness of our inner world plays in relating differently to trauma symptoms and trauma-based rumination. Then, a Christian perspective on practicing the Jesus Prayer is offered to support you in pivoting from unhelpful rumination to an awareness of Jesus' compassionate mercy. For Christians, we can relate to trauma symptoms with mercy because Jesus offers us his perfect mercy from moment to moment. Along the way, definitions, examples, and exercises are proposed for making this important shift throughout the day—from trauma-based rumination to an awareness of Jesus' merciful, compassionate presence in your inner world. Gradually, my hope is that you'll learn to see Jesus' mercy in every area of life, whether the inner or outer world. To wrap up the chapter, a real-world account of Christian awareness, consisting of Jesus' compassionate mercy applied within, is offered in the context of trauma symptoms.

A Secular Psychological Perspective

Within secular psychology, compassion is a popular concept in the 21st century. It is succinctly defined as "a strong feeling of sympathy with another person's feelings of sorrow or distress, usually involving a desire to help or comfort the person."[1] Secular psychologists have written on the topic at length in recent years. They have even embedded compassion in treatment approaches for a range of psychological struggles.[2]

DOI: 10.4324/9781003647270-7

Compassion can be applied to ourselves or others. When applied to the self,[3] we may relate to our inner world with kindness, support, and gentleness, not harshness, self-criticism, and shame. We may choose to care for and love ourselves when we hurt. We may see our suffering as part of life. We may recognize that other people are imperfect and suffer, too, which can bring us comfort in our own imperfections and suffering. Finally, we may be open and curious about our suffering by being mindful toward difficult inner experiences.

These three ingredients of self-compassion—self-kindness, common humanity, and mindfulness—have been researched extensively with the Self-Compassion Scale,[4] a measurement tool developed over two decades ago. Results have revealed a negative relationship between self-compassion and trauma symptoms.[5] This means that the more people report having compassion for themselves, the less they report symptoms of trauma.

When we have compassion for ourselves, we can relate to difficult inner experiences much differently. This is especially relevant for our discussion about trauma symptoms. Rather than trying to avoid such symptoms, which doesn't work, we can learn to relate to them with a kinder, more compassionate awareness.

To review, after a traumatic event, we may have intrusive memories (e.g., nightmares, flashbacks, vivid images) of the event. These unwanted memories may give rise to distressing emotions, like fear, anxiety, guilt, and shame. In response to these unpleasant memories and emotions, we may begin to ruminate as a cognitive avoidance strategy.[6] We may do so to think our way out of and distance ourselves from the inner distress. Yet, as we have discussed in previous chapters, this strategy seldom works. We may end up increasing the frequency and intensity of our unwanted memories and emotions[7] and tragically living life on automatic pilot.[8] When this happens, we may continue to suffer, despite our best efforts to avoid such suffering, and struggle to be present to daily life.

As an alternative to these habitual patterns of rumination and automatic pilot, we can be more aware with gentleness. We can relate to our inner world with compassion. If awareness is simply "perception or knowledge of something,"[9] we can learn to be more aware of what is going on inside of us, not stuck on automatic pilot. We can be more in touch with our thoughts, feelings, sensations, memories, and images, not disconnected and disengaged. By maintaining this awareness, we can learn to be with trauma symptoms from a place of kindness, so we don't continue to rely on rumination as a cognitive avoidance strategy. When intrusive memories and distressing emotions emerge in our inner world, we can learn to relate to them with openness. We don't inevitably need to resort to rumination.

This is where mindfulness comes in. Self-compassion is key for mindfulness, and mindfulness is key for self-compassion. To emphasize this point, some psychologists even use the language of "compassionate awareness"[10] when describing the goal of mindfulness-based practices. This compassionate awareness is the "heart of mindfulness" and "emotional attitude of mindfulness,"[11] suggesting that compassion may be the proverbial motor that powers the car of mindful change.

When we are more aware of our inner world, we can notice our thoughts, feelings, sensations, memories, and images without reacting to them in an impulsive manner. We can be more intentional about how we want to live life, rather than reacting to them with avoidance, which does not work. Not only can we maintain this awareness, but we can do so from a place of kindness, gentleness, friendliness, non-judgment, openness, and curiosity.

For example, if I have an intrusive memory of a traumatic event, a car accident that resulted in serious injuries, I can relate to it with more gentleness and kindness, not avoidance. I can relate to my mind, including all the contents in it, like trying to understand a dear friend. I can recognize that this is my mind's way of trying to process the overwhelming experience. I may even conclude that my mind is trying to protect me. Then, when difficult emotions also arise, like anxiety about getting into another car accident, I can apply self-compassion, too. I can conclude that anxiety is alerting me to potential danger. I can remind myself that it makes sense that I feel anxious after a near-death car accident. I can remember that other people, too, have gotten into violent car accidents and struggled with flashbacks and anxiety. As I learn to be with these memories and emotions, I am less likely to resort to unhelpful rumination and automatic pilot.

So, in secular clinical psychology, compassionate awareness—via mindfulness meditation—is an alternative to rumination and automatic pilot when we are struggling with trauma symptoms. By learning to be more compassionate toward our inner world, we are aware of what comes up. We can learn to ask ourselves what we need in the moment to comfort ourselves and be responsive to our own suffering.[12] This is reminiscent of a nurse asking a patient under their care what hurts and, from there, what they need. We don't resort to cognitive avoidance strategies that may only make our symptoms worse. It's sort of like how a caregiver holds, consoles, and comforts a crying infant in their arms. They don't shame the infant for crying. They don't try to force the infant to never cry again. Instead, they try to understand the crying and what it signals. They understand that infants cry to communicate. Likewise, when we have survived a traumatic event, we can compassionately maintain an awareness of our symptoms (like intrusive memories and distressing emotions) as a normal reaction to a scary, uncertain moment in life.

To engage in compassionate awareness, not rumination, toward trauma symptoms, we can use mindfulness. As an informal practice that we take with us into the real world, mindfulness really has only three basic steps: "stop, observe, and return."[13] When we are going about our day, we can stop what we are doing to observe what is going on within our inner world. From there, we can return to what we are observing when we notice our mind has inevitably drifted to another point of focus. With the observe step, we can add compassion. When it comes to our emotions, we can stop what we are doing, observe what we are feeling with compassion, and return to our feeling when our mind has drifted. By doing this three-step mindfulness activity, we are cultivating compassionate awareness of our emotions, rather than resorting to rumination as a cognitive avoidance strategy.

Within the context of trauma symptoms, I may be struggling with anxiety. This anxiety may come from a nightmare I had the night before about childhood abuse. I may anticipate that I will be abused again. Rather than ruminating about the nightmare and accompanying anxiety, I can stop what I am doing, observe my anxiety with compassion, and return to compassionately observing my anxiety when my mind drifts toward rumination. Throughout this process, I can try to relate to my anxiety like a friend, not enemy. I can try to see that the anxiety is attempting to keep me safe. I can just be with it in a nurturing, kind way. I can reassure myself I am safe, like I'd reassure an anxious child.

In support of this more accepting approach to trauma symptoms, researchers examined the relationship between mindfulness, rumination, and trauma symptoms among college students.[14] Results revealed that the more the students reported mindfulness-based skills, the less they reported ruminating. Also, the less they reported ruminating, the less they reported trauma symptoms. The authors concluded by suggesting that mindfulness can help trauma survivors relate to their trauma symptoms with greater awareness, rather than resorting to unhelpful avoidance.

Although mindfulness meditation can help us to cultivate compassionate awareness, many of its concepts and practices come to us from the Buddhist religious tradition. Therefore, Christian trauma survivors may wish to explore our own religious heritage for insights into the inner world and what to do about psychological suffering.

A Christian Perspective

From a Christian viewpoint, Jesus offers us his mercy—or his compassionate, kind responsiveness—from moment to moment. We can call on him to soothe and comfort us during both inner and outer struggles. In the gospels some 2,000 years ago, many individuals called on Jesus for mercy.[15] With these pleas, those who needed Jesus' healing called on him to offer his compassionate reply. As another example, writing almost 1,000 years ago, the French Christian writer and abbot Bernard of Clairvaux passionately explained in his commentary on the Song of Songs that we should call on the name of Jesus, which is like medicine when we are sad, afraid, discouraged, or suffering in any other way.[16]

Returning to the New Testament, the Greek word for mercy, *eleos*, is used many times by biblical authors. It captures the need for compassion, as both an emotional and behavioral response, for individuals who are distressed.[17] With this type of mercy, though, Christian trauma survivors aren't solely responsible for conjuring up self-compassion. Instead, we can call on Jesus' name. He is with us when we struggle with trauma symptoms. So, a Christian alternative to individualized mindfulness meditation for compassionate awareness is to relationally call on the name of Jesus to cultivate merciful awareness. This merciful awareness begins with Jesus because he is a God of compassion. Then, we can extend his merciful compassion to ourselves during psychological suffering.

One example of *eleos* comes to us from Hebrews 4. There, we read that we can directly approach Jesus, who offers us his mercy "to help us in our time of need." Because Jesus lived a fully human life filled with psychological suffering, he empathizes with our vulnerabilities and weaknesses.[18] This means that Jesus understands our pain because he, too, suffered as a human being. It is vitally important, then, for Christian trauma survivors to spend time with him, especially when we are weighed down by trauma symptoms. He gets us, and he wants to respond to our needs with his compassionate mercy. If compassion is simply defined as being moved by suffering and responsive to suffering,[19] Jesus understands our trauma-based suffering, is moved by it, and wants to soothe and comfort us during it.

For Christian trauma survivors, compassionate awareness of our trauma symptoms involves calling on the name of Jesus. As we learn to recognize that Jesus is dwelling within, we can begin to feel his compassionate, merciful presence. As we feel his presence, we can begin to have compassion for ourselves the way he has compassion for us, including our trauma symptoms. Whereas mindfulness meditation is an individualized way to have compassionate awareness for our trauma symptoms, Christian prayer practices are a relational strategy to recognize God's compassionate presence, then extend this compassion to ourselves and others.

One such way to call on Jesus' compassion and mercy is with the Jesus Prayer. There are several versions of this famous, centuries-old prayer. The longest version is "Lord Jesus Christ, Son of God, have mercy on me, a sinner." The shorter version, which I personally prefer, is "Lord Jesus Christ, have mercy on me." Possibly the shortest version is "Lord Jesus, have mercy." Or we may simply call on the name of Jesus, as in "Jesus."

Scripturally, the prayer was likely inspired by the many times in the gospels that people asked Jesus for mercy.[20] It may have also been influenced by the Apostle Paul's instructions to "pray continually."[21] By calling on Jesus' name with this simple prayer, we find several important ingredients.[22]

First, we are asking Jesus for his mercy, or compassionate understanding and responsiveness, in our distressing time of need. Early Christian writers have pointed out that the Greek word for mercy, *eleos*, is like the Greek word for olive oil, *elaion*.[23] During Jesus' time, olive oil was used as an ointment to soothe and heal wounds. This means that we are asking Jesus to soothe our wounds when we ask for his mercy.

Second, by repeating the prayer, we are engaging in "monologic prayer." This is the repetition of a word or short phrase to focus a distracted, chaotic, distressed mind.[24] As we slowly and gently meditate on the words, there may be a calming, settling effect.

Finally, the Jesus Prayer can help us to remain watchful, or aware, of the inner world, the Greek word *nepsis*.[25] When we repeat the prayer within, we are able to maintain a greater awareness of all the different thoughts that come and go. We notice them, then gently return to the prayer. Over time, we gain a greater awareness of the thoughts that pull us away and distract us from our relationship with God.

To consolidate this understanding, the Jesus Prayer offers us a Christian alternative to mindfulness to maintain compassionate awareness of the inner world. As we recite the prayer, we are learning to rest in Jesus' compassionate mercy, which we can, in turn, apply to ourselves. Rather than ruminating to cognitively avoid difficult trauma-related memories and emotions, we can call on Jesus to soothe our wounds and be with us in our time of need. We are not alone when we suffer, since Jesus knows what it means to suffer. As we repeat the words of the prayer, they can also have a calming, settling impact on our ruminative mind. Over time, we can become more watchful and aware of inner experiences like unwanted memories and images and distressing emotions. Rather than ruminating, we can maintain compassionate, merciful awareness toward them because Jesus is also dwelling within.

Interestingly, the Jesus Prayer has also been called the "prayer of the heart" because we are imagining we are saying the prayer deep within, where Jesus resides. Because Jesus dwells within our heart, the difficult thoughts, feelings, sensations, memories, and images that swirl around our mind will not harm us. It's as if we are scuba diving with Jesus and calmly and safely sitting at the bottom of the ocean.[26] Although we can look up to the surface of the water and see choppy waves, floating seaweed, boats, and other distractions, they need not harm us because we are with our Lord and Savior.[27] Likewise, we can simply watch our inner world with a bit more distance and compassionate, merciful awareness because Jesus gets us and is responsive to our psychological struggles. We need not engage in ruminative thinking as a form of avoidance because we can watch trauma symptoms with open curiosity and a trustworthy ally in Jesus.

As a reminder, I recently researched with several colleagues the use of Christian meditation for trauma-based rumination.[28] For one of the four weeks of the four-week program, participants were instructed to practice the Jesus

Prayer to cultivate compassionate awareness of trauma symptoms. Upon conclusion of the study, participants reported a reduction in trauma-based rumination and trauma symptoms and an increase in awareness as a Christian skill.

Prior to this study, a colleague and I researched the Jesus Prayer on its own as an intervention for daily stress among college students.[29] The students were advised to practice the prayer daily over a two-week period. When the study ended, we found that, overall, students reported a reduction in daily stress. These results suggest that the Jesus Prayer holds promise as a Christian alternative to mindfulness meditation for psychological suffering. Let's now turn to an integrative understanding of the problem of trauma symptoms and solution of compassionate awareness, then shift toward the actual practice of the Jesus Prayer for trauma-based rumination and other trauma symptoms.

An Integrative Perspective: Shifting from Trauma-Based Rumination to Practicing the Jesus Prayer

To provide an integrative understanding, both mindfulness meditation and the Jesus Prayer can help us to relate differently to our inner struggles. Rather than shaming ourselves for trauma-based rumination and other trauma symptoms, we can recognize, with compassionate awareness, that these inner experiences are a response to traumatic events and living in a fallen, broken world. However, rather than unilaterally attempting to conjure up compassion for the self, a self-generated compassion, Christians can call upon Jesus for his merciful reply, an Other-generated compassion. We are not alone to face our inner struggles in isolation. Jesus, who took on human form and empathizes with our weaknesses and struggles, gets us. He wants to soothe and comfort us as wounded trauma survivors. Let's now pivot to the exercises in this chapter to help you relate differently to your trauma symptoms as you move toward healing with Jesus by your side.

Exercises

Self-Monitoring Log

To begin the exercises in this chapter, please spend a day logging your experiences of intrusive memories, distressing emotions, unhelpful rumination, and efforts to maintain compassionate awareness of your inner world (see Table 7.1). Like the previous two chapters, this will give you a better sense of your current functioning. It will help you better understand when these trauma

TABLE 7.1
Self-Monitoring Log

	Intrusive Memories/ Images/ Dreams	Distressing Emotions (Fear, Anxiety, Sadness, Anger, Guilt, Shame, Helplessness, Other)	Type of Unhelpful Rumination ("Why" Questions, "What If" Questions, Meaning of Event, Antecedents or Consequences of Event, Future Events)	Coping Strategy to Maintain Compassionate Awareness of Inner World (Journaling, Praying, Spending Time in Solitude and Silence)/Level of Success
6:00 a.m.	*Flashback of active combat.*	*Overwhelming fear and anxiety.*	*What if I'm in danger again?*	*Trying to journal to sort out my thoughts and feelings/not successful.*
7:00 a.m.				
8:00 a.m.				
9:00 a.m.				
10:00 a.m.				
11:00 a.m.				
12:00 p.m.				
1:00 p.m.				
2:00 p.m.				
3:00 p.m.				
4:00 p.m.				
5:00 p.m.				
6:00 p.m.				
7:00 p.m.				
8:00 p.m.				
9:00 p.m.				
10:00 p.m.				
11:00 p.m.				

symptoms occur throughout the day, how you attempt to cope with them by staying compassionately aware of your inner world, and your level of success in doing so as you continue with the chapter's activities. I've added an example in the 6:00 a.m. row to get you started. Please use extra paper if needed.

Like the last two chapters, once you have recorded your answers for a day, please respond to the below questions as best you can. Please use extra paper if needed.

1. What relationship, if any, emerged between your possible intrusive memories, distressing emotions, unhelpful ruminations, and coping strategies/level of success? Did you notice a certain pattern that materialized?

    _____

    _____

    _____

    _____

    _____

    _____

2. What types of rumination, if any, did you struggle with in response to possible intrusive memories and distressing emotions?

    _____

    _____

    _____

    _____

    _____

3. How, if at all, did you attempt to maintain compassionate awareness of your inner world? Were you successful? Why or why not?

    _____

    _____

    _____

    _____

    _____

    _____

Like the last two chapters, the goal is to begin to increase your self-awareness of the relationship between intrusive memories, distressing emotions, rumination, and coping strategies (this time focusing on maintaining compassionate awareness of the inner world). This burgeoning awareness can help you prepare for a different, more intentional strategy—praying the Jesus Prayer. Let's turn now to a spiritual exercise drawn from the Orthodox Christian tradition, where Jesus is offering you his mercy within your inner world.

Developing Christian Awareness with the Jesus Prayer[30]

In this chapter, you will be formally practicing the Jesus Prayer, first introduced in prior chapters, for 10 minutes. Try to set a specific time each day. Find a quiet environment that is free from distractions. Put away your smart phone or any other electronic device to spend this time with Jesus. You can also follow along with the audio file if you'd like: www.routledge.com/9781041088608.

1. Begin to slowly, gently, and within recite the Jesus Prayer.
2. Inhale "Lord Jesus Christ," then exhale "have mercy on me."
3. Imagine you are saying the prayer within the center of your being, or heart.
4. When your mind inevitably wanders to something else, such as trauma-based intrusive memories, distressing emotions, or rumination, compassionately and mercifully return to the prayer.
5. As you continue to practice, ask Jesus to soothe your inner experience, whatever it may be, with his perfect, compassionate mercy.
6. Conclude the practice by thanking Jesus for offering you his compassionate mercy right here and now. Ask him to continue to help you call on his name for soothing comfort during trauma-based rumination and other trauma symptoms.

Upon conclusion of the 10-minute practice, try to journal for a few minutes about your experience with the below questions (please use extra paper if needed):

1. What was it like to recite the Jesus Prayer to maintain compassionate, merciful awareness of the inner world?

_____

_____

_____

_____

_____

_____

2. How well were you able to maintain compassionate, merciful awareness of your inner world as you recited the prayer?

_____

_____

_____

_____

_____

_____

3. What was it like to call upon Jesus for his compassionate mercy in response to trauma-based rumination and other trauma symptoms?

_____

_____

_____

_____

_____

_____

4. How well did practicing the Jesus Prayer help you shift from intrusive memories, distressing emotions, and/or trauma-based rumination if these experiences emerged?

_____

_____

_____

_____

_____

_____

5. How can you set aside time to recite the Jesus Prayer formally in daily life? How can you also recite the prayer spontaneously throughout the day when you get distracted with intrusive memories, distressing emotions, or trauma-based rumination?

_____

_____

_____

_____

_____

_____

Remember that you can recite the Jesus Prayer both formally, in solitude and silence, and informally throughout the day. In either case, you are learning to notice when you get caught in cycles of trauma-based rumination, then gently and lovingly call on Jesus for his compassionate mercy. As you do so, you are learning to maintain compassionate, merciful awareness of the inner world, including trauma-based symptoms. With this awareness, you are inviting Jesus to be with you during your inner struggles. Let's now turn to a case example to bring the Jesus Prayer to life prior to concluding the chapter.

Case Example

Right out of high school, Marvin joined the military. Growing up, he was part of a long line of family members who served in the U.S. Army. Excited to serve, Marvin was eventually stationed in a part of the world that was war-torn and violent. Although he was confident in his training, a part of him was highly anxious and uncertain about his future.

After a six-month period of serving overseas, Marvin witnessed a fellow soldier die for the first time. This experience left him shaken. Although Marvin grew up as a committed Christian, and believed that God cared for him, he began to doubt God's presence amid the violence he witnessed daily.

Upon returning to civilian life, Marvin had a really hard time adjusting. He had regular nightmares of helplessly watching his friend die. He also struggled to develop close friendships because no one else seemed to understand what it was like to witness such violence and suffering. Marvin also suffered from overwhelming anxiety. He predicted that he would inevitably see other people die in his life, something he couldn't accept. He also suffered from debilitating guilt. He convinced himself that he could have done more to save his friend prior to his friend's passing.

To make matters worse, Marvin began to ruminate in response to his unwanted nightmares and emotional distress. He questioned why these things happened to him. He also repeatedly asked why God would allow—or possibly cause—such evil and violence in the world. Unfortunately, his rumination only increased the frequency and intensity of his trauma symptoms.

One morning roughly a year after he returned home, Marvin had had enough. He was exhausted, demoralized, and lonely. He had no real friends, and he was not part of a church community. His apartment was orderly, yet his inner world was a mess. He promised himself he would reach out to a Christian therapist to get help.

Upon making an appointment with a local Christian therapist, Dr. McGuire, he began to feel better. Entering her office, he immediately realized he needed to be more intentional about dealing with his trauma symptoms. They weren't going away, and he needed to trust someone to teach him a set of skills to relate differently to his distress.

After learning more about Marvin's family background, military history, religious/spiritual functioning, and current symptoms, Dr. McGuire diagnosed Marvin with posttraumatic stress disorder (PTSD). As one of the first steps, she helped him to feel safe with her by attempting to understand his pain. Although she couldn't promise any sort of outcome to treatment, she was committed to walking with him through his suffering. She also helped Marvin to see that his rumination was an understandable way to avoid his intense memories and unpleasant emotions. Yet, she explained, the rumination may have been making his symptoms worse. Therefore, Dr. McGuire proposed an alternative solution—to learn to be more compassionate, with greater kindness and awareness, to his symptoms.

Because Marvin identified as a Christian and wanted to get help from a Christian perspective, Dr. McGuire suggested the Jesus Prayer as an intervention to help Marvin relate to his trauma symptoms with more compassion and mercy. To get Marvin started, she proposed practicing it with him in one of their sessions, which he agreed to do. As he began to practice, with Dr. McGuire in the room, he immediately began to cry. He had longed for Jesus to comfort him in his experience of brokenness. He was lonely, and he needed soothing relief. Marvin was especially drawn to the idea that Jesus, too, had experienced trauma while on the cross. This brought him comfort in knowing that Jesus understood his battle with trauma symptoms. And Jesus' trauma had a purpose. The Son of God used this traumatic experience to reconcile himself to those who put their faith in him.

After this session, Marvin began to practice the Jesus Prayer on his own. Gradually, he was able to relate differently to his trauma symptoms, especially the intrusive flashbacks and nightmares. Although they didn't fully go away, their intensity lessened. He was able to see them as a normal response to the traumatizing experience of watching his friend die right in front of him. With more compassion and mercy, he was able to cry out to Jesus to comfort him in his distress, which seemed to settle and calm him down. This relational approach to his trauma symptoms was especially powerful for Marvin because he had erroneously convinced himself that God had abandoned him. Although he still didn't have all the answers when it came to why God would allow or cause so much suffering in the world, he could trust that Jesus understood trauma and was there for him as much-needed medicine for his body and soul.

Conclusion

In this chapter, you learned about the importance of compassionate awareness. With compassion, we can relate to trauma symptoms with more kindness, gentleness, and open curiosity. We need not resort to compulsive rumination as an avoidance strategy, which may only make our trauma-related distress worse.

Although mindfulness meditation is one helpful strategy for cultivating compassionate awareness, it comes from the Buddhist religious tradition. And it's an individualized approach, meaning it is meant to be practiced alone. For Christians, we have our own religious heritage to draw from. This heritage tells us we have Jesus as both the Son of God and someone who fully lived a human life, filled with temptations and suffering.

By calling on the name of Jesus, as Christian trauma survivors, we can learn to receive Jesus' merciful, compassionate reply, which can help us to be more aware of our trauma symptoms. Rather than getting stuck in endless cycles of rumination, we can recite the Jesus Prayer to calm the mind, watch the contents of the mind with a bit more distance, and, ultimately, have compassion for ourselves. This is because we follow, worship, and serve a God of compassion. Now that we have covered chapters on Christian attention, Christian focus on the present moment, and Christian awareness, I'd like us to conclude the workbook with a chapter on Christian acceptance. By learning to be more accepting of trauma symptoms, we will let go of the temptation to use rumination as a form of avoidance. Instead of ending up exhausted and demoralized, Christian loving acceptance can help us to live life again as trauma survivors.

Notes

 1 APA Dictionary (n.d.d).
 2 Gilbert (2010).
 3 This paragraph on self-compassion is based on a review of Neff (2003).
 4 Neff (2003).
 5 Winders et al. (2020).
 6 Michael et al. (2007).
 7 Michael et al. (2007).
 8 Segal et al. (2012).
 9 APA Dictionary (n.d.c).
10 Germer and Neff (2018).
11 Germer and Neff (2015).
12 Germer and Neff (2015).
13 Germer (2009).
14 Im and Follette (2016).
15 See, for example, Mark 10:47–48 and Luke 18:38–41.
16 Saint Bernard of Clairvaux (2016).
17 Bible Hub (n.d.).
18 See Hebrews 4:14–16.
19 Gilbert (2010).
20 See, again, Mark 10:47–48 and Luke 18:38–41.
21 1 Thessalonians 5:16–18.
22 Ware (2014).
23 Ware (2014).
24 Ware (2014).
25 Wellington (2020).
26 Bourgeault (2004).
27 Bourgeault (2004).
28 Knabb et al. (2022).
29 Knabb and Vazquez (2018).
30 This exercise is based on a review of Talbot (2013), with portions from Knabb et al. (2019c).

CHAPTER 8

Skill 4
Christian Acceptance

Introduction

In the final skill-based chapter, we'll unpack Christian acceptance. First, we'll cover a secular psychological perspective on acceptance. This skill has been widely researched in contemporary clinical psychology and plays an important function in effectively responding to trauma symptoms and trauma-based rumination. Next, we'll explore a Christian view on the role that the daily examen, a Jesuit spiritual practice developed in the 16th century, can play in helping you turn from unhelpful rumination to an awareness of God's loving and caring activity in daily life. Throughout the chapter, definitions, examples, exercises, and a real-world example of Christian acceptance are offered to aid you on your journey toward psychological and spiritual healing.

A Secular Psychological Perspective

Within 21st century secular clinical psychology, the term acceptance is quite popular. It refers to both a "favorable attitude toward an idea, situation, person, or group" and a "receptive, non-judgmental attitude."[1] When applied to the inner world, acceptance means "opening up to our inner experiences (thoughts, images, memories, feelings, emotions, urges, impulses, sensations) and allowing them to be as they are, regardless of whether they are pleasant or

DOI: 10.4324/9781003647270-8

painful."[2] Some clinical psychologists have even pointed out that, at its root, acceptance means to "take what is offered" or willingly receive.[3] It means to work with what is already there, not fight against reality. This reality is that, living in a fallen world, our imperfect and vulnerable human mind is bound to generate difficult inner experiences. It is unrealistic to expect that we will never have unpleasant thoughts, feelings, sensations, memories, and images.

So, acceptance is about embracing the reality of what's already there—unpleasant inner experiences. Instead of fighting reality, which can take up all our energy and leave us distracted and discouraged, we accept the inner world so we can live life to the fullest in the outer world. We can have a positive attitude toward our inner world, even when our inner experiences are painful. But why is it important to accept, not avoid, our inner experiences? Why not try to avoid them at all costs, especially when they cause us so much distress? To avoid seems only natural. Who would *want* to embrace inner pain?

Secular clinical psychologists have been researching the psychological phenomenon called experiential avoidance for some time now. Experiential avoidance, first introduced in prior chapters, involves trying to avoid, suppress, distract ourselves from, numb ourselves from, or deny unpleasant inner experiences, whether thoughts, feelings, sensations, memories, or images.[4]

The problem with experiential avoidance is that it doesn't work. Instead of ridding ourselves of the difficult inner experiences, we end up distracting ourselves from living the life we want to live. And we end up being exhausted and discouraged because our efforts to avoid and rid are in vain. So, we end up continuing to struggle with the original inner pain. We also have a hard time living a life of meaning and purpose. Because of this, acceptance, not avoidance, is preferred for pragmatic, practical purposes—experiential avoidance is an ineffective coping strategy. Whether we try to distract ourselves with social media, numb ourselves with drugs, alcohol, or food, or use some other unhelpful avoidance strategy, we end up feeling demoralized and hopeless.

In support of the idea that experiential avoidance doesn't work, in the context of trauma, researchers have found that it is positively linked to trauma symptoms.[5] This means that people who report they are more likely to try to avoid their difficult inner experiences are more likely to also report trauma symptoms. So, even though avoidance is meant to rid us of trauma, it has the opposite effect. Adding rumination to the discussion, researchers have found that as trauma survivors report more struggles with rumination, they report greater efforts to avoid their inner struggles.[6] And the more they try to avoid their inner struggles, the more trauma symptoms they report.[7] This means that rumination is meant to avoid, but it ends up leading to more struggles with trauma.

These research findings suggest that we may use rumination to avoid painful thoughts, feelings, sensations, memories, and images. Yet, avoidance as a go-to coping strategy may only lead to more trauma-related suffering. This is because trauma-based rumination often involves asking "Why" and "What if" questions about the causes and consequences of the traumatic event.[8] When we repeatedly ask such questions, we don't try to make sense of what happened and how we felt and currently feel. In other words, we don't process the traumatic event in a healthy way. Rather, we end up "spinning our wheels" by cognitively going over and over often unanswerable questions. Based on these findings, acceptance may be an effective alternative to avoidance, since avoidance doesn't give us what we are hoping for—permanent symptom relief from trauma. Acceptance may help us to process what happened and how we feel about it in a way that is authentic and necessary.

For many trauma survivors, though, acceptance doesn't seem very helpful when we understandably want to avoid mental pain in the inner world. Why wouldn't we? We also understandably want to avoid any sense of danger in the external world for both survival and to live a pleasurable life. Again, why wouldn't we?

When we are faced with danger in the outer world, fight-or-flight can kick in. This is the brain's way of responding to a dangerous situation, both physically and psychologically. Our heart rate increases, we release hormones like adrenaline, we breathe more quickly, and we may experience increased fear and anxiety. Although this natural sympathetic nervous system activity is helpful for responding to threats in the outer world, we can erroneously apply it to the inner world.[9] Unfortunately, trying to fight with trauma symptoms or flee from them doesn't work, and we end up feeling exhausted, frustrated, and distracted.

Here's where love comes into play. Many secular psychologists emphasize the importance of *loving* acceptance, not mere acceptance, toward our difficult inner experiences.[10] It's not just that we willingly receive inner pain from a place of non-judgment and neutrality. Instead, we have an attitude of loving acceptance toward such pain. Love, in this context, means benevolent intentions toward our symptoms. We have concern and good will toward our inner world. This contrasts with aggression, shame, or self-criticism toward our psychological suffering. Loving acceptance, not violence and harshness, is the preferred approach to our pain.

Yes, we accept our inner pain because avoidance doesn't work. However, beyond mere acceptance, we lovingly embrace our inner world. But why, ultimately, should we try to love our most difficult inner struggles as an approach to life? Here's where we can return to our prior discussions on mindfulness as both an attitude toward all of life (whether the inner or outer world) and meditative practice.

If mindfulness is simply defined as "awareness of present experience with loving acceptance,"[11] it's not just attention, focus on the present moment, and awareness that are important skills. (These are certainly key and have been covered from both secular and Christian perspectives in the last three skill-based chapters.) We also need to be kind, open, and curious toward whatever we experience within the mind.[12] We can approach our mind like we are training a puppy.[13] When we train a puppy, we don't yell at it when it wanders off, urinates on the carpet, or cries at night. Instead, we recognize that puppies engage in these types of behavior. We accept them because they are normal from a developmental perspective. We understand what puppies do because we understand they are vulnerable puppies that need our care and affection. We still love the puppy and treat it with kindness even when it is difficult. Likewise, we can approach the mind like a puppy. When we struggle with intrusive memories, difficult emotions, and rumination, we can recognize this is our mind's response to a traumatic event. We can understand our mind and treat it with kindness, much like the puppy. This contrasts with being harsh, shaming, and judgmental, which does not help us when training a puppy or when our trauma symptoms won't go away. This loving attitude toward our trauma also contrasts with avoidance, which does not work in the long run.

We can learn to practice loving acceptance toward trauma-based thoughts (e.g., rumination, worry), feelings (e.g., fear, anxiety, guilt, shame, anger), and memories and images (e.g., flashbacks, nightmares) formally via mindfulness meditation.[14] One such formal meditative practice is called "Stepping into Fear."[15] It involves trying to locate the sensation of anxiety in the body. Once we locate it, we can try to paradoxically make it grow. We do this so we can work with it in a new, more loving way. From there, we can simply be with the anxiety to get used to it. As we sit with the anxiety, we can embrace it with an attitude of openness, kindness, and love. We can soften the bodily area in which we are feeling the anxiety, then allow whatever accompanying thoughts are there, then love the anxiety by repeating "soften, allow, and love."[16] We can treat the anxiety like we would a hurting, vulnerable child, which changes our experience of it.[17] Rather than shaming, judging, or avoiding, we embrace the child and soothe and comfort them. Gradually, anxiety becomes something we nurture, not hate.

To summarize, loving acceptance is the alternative to avoidance because avoidance doesn't work in eliminating our inner pain. We can also accept our inner struggles with kindness and openness because avoidance distracts us from living a life of meaning and purpose. This is especially true when our trauma symptoms don't go away. Although they are certainly difficult, as trauma survivors, we can end up overly relying on rumination to distance ourselves from unwanted memories and painful emotions. This may only make such memories and emotions worse.[18] Although we need fight-or-flight and the sympathetic nervous system in the outer world, fight or flight doesn't work as effectively in the inner world. By accepting our trauma symptoms with love, we can pivot away from automatic pilot and toward being more fully engaged with life.[19] We can decide what we want to do because we are not distracted by inner pain and preoccupied with avoidance. To practice loving acceptance, mindfulness meditation can be helpful. Yet, it comes to us from the Buddhist religious tradition. Therefore, as Christian trauma survivors, I'd like us to now explore a Christian alternative to loving acceptance within mindfulness meditation.

A Christian Perspective

Like non-Christian trauma survivors, Christians can certainly learn to accept our inner world because avoidance doesn't work. This pragmatic approach to accepting internal pain can be helpful in living the kind of life we want to live since we are less distracted and preoccupied. This contrasts with using rumination as a form of avoidance—with its accompanying automatic pilot[20]—when we struggle with unwanted memories and emotions.[21] When we ruminate about the event, we aren't trying to process what happened or the emotions we felt both then and now. Rather, we are asking unhelpful "Why" ("Why did it happen?") and "What if" ("What if it happens again?" "What if I continue to feel anxious?") questions about the causes and consequences of the event that may increase the frequency of intrusive memories and distressing emotions like anxiety.[22]

As Christians, we also have another, more important reason for accepting inner experiences—God's providence. This biblical concept, revisited from Chapter 3, can be defined as "God's benevolent and wise superintendence of His creation."[23] God's providence means he is personally, purposefully, lovingly, wisely, and actively involved in guiding his creation and everything and everyone in it.[24] He is intentionally working in and through large events and small events. He is actively working in and through the life of humans, whether the external, social world or humans' inner psychological world. As he governs, God's actions are infinitely good, wise, and powerful. This means that God has Christians' best intentions in mind, knows all possible outcomes, and has the power to carry out the best possible outcomes.

This important Christian concept has been written on extensively over the last several hundred years. God's providence is especially salient when we consider traumatic events in the outer world and our psychological response in the inner world. Although we don't fully understand all that happens to us in life, we can trust that God is working things out for his good.[25] In other words, there is a mystery to God's providence that we'll never fully understand on this side of heaven.[26] So, instead of ruminating to come up with "Why" answers on our own, we can learn to trust in his benevolent plan. God's providential care extends to our inner world, too.[27] God dwells within the inner life of Christians. Because he dwells within, we are not alone to face our trauma symptoms. Instead, God is personally and actively with us as we think, feel, sense, imagine, and remember. He is loving us within from moment to moment.

Whereas secular clinical psychologists advocate for loving acceptance toward our difficult inner experiences for pragmatic reasons—because avoidance doesn't work and prevents us from processing traumatic events in a healthy manner—Christian trauma survivors can also trust in God's active, purposeful, loving, and wise care. Like Joseph being sold as a slave in Genesis (i.e., "You intended to harm me, but God intended it for good")[28] and the Apostle Paul's teaching that "all things God works for the good of those who love him,"[29] we can find a deeper contentment in life's most challenging situations.[30] Although this is by no means an easy thing to do, like loving acceptance with mindfulness, we can learn to accept because avoidance doesn't work. As Christians, we can also accept because we know God is infinitely loving, wise, powerful, and present. He is with us to help us face and process what happened and how we feel about it.

To capture God's providence in more detail, I believe the Belgic confession can be helpful. This document was written in the 1500s to capture who God is from a Protestant perspective. In Article 13,[31] we read about God's providence:

> We believe that the same God, after he had created all things, did not forsake them, or give them up to fortune or chance, but that he rules and governs them according to his holy will, so that nothing happens in this world without his appointment: nevertheless, God neither is the author of, nor can be charged with, the sins which are committed. For his power and goodness are so great and incomprehensible, that he orders and executes his work in the most excellent and just manner, even then, when devils and wicked men act unjustly. And, as to what he [does] surpassing human understanding, we will not curiously inquire into, farther than our capacity will admit of; but with the greatest humility and reverence adore the righteous judgments of God, which are hid from us, contenting ourselves that we are disciples of Christ, to learn only those things which he has revealed to us in his Word, without transgressing these limits. This doctrine affords us unspeakable consolation, since we are taught thereby that nothing can befall us by chance, but by the direction of our most gracious and heavenly Father; who watches over us with a paternal care, keeping all creatures so under his power, that not a hair of our head (for they are all numbered), nor a sparrow, can fall to the ground, without the will of our Father, in whom we do entirely trust; being persuaded, that he so restrains the devil and all our enemies, that without his will and permission, they cannot hurt us.

This lengthy explanation suggests that God is personal and purposeful in his actions, rather than leaving events to chance in a removed manner. He is a benevolent governor who carries out his perfect will. Although he is not responsible for human sin, he works *all* things out for good. Because of this, we can trust in his perfect care, rather than getting stuck in endless patterns of rumination (e.g., "Why" and "What if" questions). We can find comfort in knowing that, beyond simply accepting trauma-related experiences and symptoms because avoidance doesn't work, we can lovingly accept them because we have a loving, wise, powerful, and present Father who is helping us process traumatic events and trauma symptoms.

When we experience trauma-related intrusive images and painful emotions, we may begin to ruminate as a cognitive avoidance strategy.[32] We may start to ask "Why" and "What if" questions to distance ourselves from the distressing images and feelings. We may ask these questions in a perseverative manner to focus on the causes and consequences of the event.[33] Yet, as we've talked about previously, this doesn't work. Rumination may make our unwanted memories and emotions worse[34] and leave us distracted on automatic pilot.[35] It may prevent us from processing the event by staying in touch with what we felt and feel about it. When we notice we are stuck with ruminative thinking, we can learn to lovingly accept our unpleasant inner world because God's providence extends to what we experience within. He is with us to process the event itself and what we feel about it.

Several hundred years ago, a Jesuit Christian author wrote about the importance of surrendering to God's providence to attain a more enduring happiness in life. Although surrender is often used negatively in contemporary society, like when a country reluctantly surrenders to another country during war, here, it is used positively. Surrendering to God, for Christians, simply means to stop fighting against him. It means we stop fighting against God's loving activity and comforting presence. This perspective is still relevant for us today. In *Trustful Surrender to Divine Providence*, Claude de la Colombiere suggested we can yield to God's loving, wise care to cultivate and maintain a deeper peace in life during both inner and outer suffering.[36] The author explained:

> The happiness of the person whose will is entirely submitted to God's is constant, unchangeable and endless. No fear comes to disturb it for no accident can destroy it. He is like a man seated on a rock in the middle of the ocean who looks on the fury of the waves without dismay and can amuse himself watching and counting them as they roar and break at his feet. Whether the sea is calm or rough, whichever way the waves are carried by the wind is a matter of indifference to him, for the place where he is is firm and unshakable.[37]

As Christian trauma survivors, we can trust in God's benevolent care to relate to our inner world with loving acceptance. We can face, not avoid, our trauma symptoms because he is also present within. We can trust that he will provide.

In support of this strategy, Jesus said, "Do not worry."[38] Jesus taught us that we don't have to worry because God will provide for us. He pointed to the birds and lilies to make the point that, if God provides for them, he will certainly take care of us. With trauma, we may be ruminating about the past traumatic event or worrying about another traumatic event happening in the future. We may be ruminating about the causes or consequences of the event. When we get stuck in these cycles, we can learn to shift toward a greater awareness of God's loving care. We can confidently rest "on a rock in the middle of the ocean" as we look upon the "fury of [life's] waves,"[39] knowing God is the author of all. We can ask God to be with us in our most difficult memories and emotions.

In the Jesuit Christian tradition, "Finding God in all things" is a famous saying (first introduced in a prior chapter). This means that we can recognize God's providence in both the large and small experiences of the day. We can find God in the outer world with our human interactions and inner world with our psychological functioning. We can use the Christian skills of attention (attending to what God is doing), focus on the present moment (recognizing God's activity in the here-and-now), awareness (acknowledging God's merciful compassion within our inner world), and, as the theme for this chapter, acceptance (surrendering to God's loving, wise, and powerful care within). But how might we learn to do so in response to traumatic events in the outer world and trauma symptoms in the inner world?

We can start by practicing the daily examen, first introduced in prior chapters. This is a meditative practice that comes to us from the Jesuit tradition. It is used to develop a greater acceptance of God's moment-by-moment presence in our emotional world. In Ignatius of Loyola's *Spiritual Exercises*, written several hundred years ago, he offered this practice to deepen our trust in God. This practice commonly involves a few basic steps to reflect on the day and "find God in all things." Among the steps, we thank him for being present, connect to and accept our emotions, ask God to reveal his activity in our emotions, and ask God to be with us as we look to tomorrow.[40] As we increasingly find God in the more painful feelings we experience daily, we gradually learn to relate differently to your inner world. We move toward accepting—rather than avoiding—our emotions because God is using them to communicate with us and reveal his presence.[41]

In the context of trauma-related intrusive memories and distressing emotions, we are asking the question, "What are you revealing to me in and through these inner experiences, God?" We are shifting from a causal view, which blames God, to a functional view, which attempts to discern God's activity in our emotional pain.[42] During these moments of pain, God is revealing our need for him for consolation and comfort. We can, through our psychological suffering, learn to trust in him because he is infinitely loving, wise, powerful, and present. We can also begin to process the traumatic event and our emotional reactions to it by accepting God's loving presence within. Because he dwells within, we can lean into, not avoid, our trauma symptoms to heal from them.

One form of the daily examen emphasizes exploring our "fears, attachments, [need for] control, and entitlements" (*FACE*).[43] In the context of trauma, we can ask God to reveal to us what fears we have throughout the day and what he is revealing to us in them. We can also ask him about the things we are clinging or attaching ourselves to and what he is revealing to us in them. Next, we can ask God what we are trying to control throughout the day and what he is revealing to us in this need for control. Lastly, we can ask God to reveal what entitlements we may have about how life should be and what he is revealing to us in them. As we try to better understand these vulnerabilities, we can ask God to reveal his providential care in the middle of them. When we examine our inner world with God, we are moving toward loving acceptance of the inner world. If God dwells within, we do not need to ruminate as a cognitive avoidance strategy. Instead, we can ask God what he's up to as he reveals our fears, attachments, desire for control, and entitlements, explained below in the daily examen practice.

I've researched this strategy of Christian acceptance with several colleagues, described in previous chapters. Several years ago, we examined the use of Christian meditation for trauma-based rumination.[44] For one of the four weeks of the four-week program, participants were instructed to practice the daily examen to develop loving acceptance, rather than engaging in ruminative avoidance, toward trauma symptoms. After the four-week study concluded, participants reported a reduction in trauma-based rumination and trauma symptoms and an increase in acceptance as a Christian skill.

To offer one more study, two colleagues and I researched Christian spiritual practices (like the Jesus Prayer, mentioned last chapter) for chronic worriers,[45] briefly mentioned in a prior chapter. We argued that Christian chronic worriers can learn to surrender to God's providence as an antidote to worry. Worry, from our perspective, is Christians' unilateral attempt to attain certainty and avoid anxiety in an ambiguous, fallen world. We gave participants questionnaires that measured their beliefs about God's providence, their ability to surrender to God's will, their ability to accept the uncertainties of life, and worry. The results of this initial study revealed that the Christians who reported they were able to surrender to God's providence were more likely to accept the uncertainties of life and, consequently, less likely to worry. From there, we administered an eight-week intervention that consisted of daily spiritual practices (like the Jesus Prayer) to surrender to God's providence during uncertainty and worry. The pilot results of this study revealed that Christians reported less uncertainty and worry after engaging in daily spiritual practices that involved surrendering to God's providence. These results suggest that surrendering to God's loving care can be helpful when we get stuck in repetitive patterns of thinking like worry (and rumination). Before we turn to the two exercises for the chapter, I'd like to offer an integrative understanding of the problem and solution to consolidate our learning.

An Integrative Perspective: Shifting from Trauma-Based Rumination to Christian Acceptance

To provide an integrative viewpoint, loving acceptance comes to us from mindfulness (as either an informal approach to life or formal meditative practice). With loving acceptance, we are learning to relate to our inner world with more kindness and openness. This is because avoidance doesn't work. When we prioritize avoidance, we may end up ruminating to distance ourselves from trauma-related intrusive memories and emotions. However, rumination may increase the frequency and intensity of the memories and emotions we are trying to rid ourselves of.[46] Therefore, instead of avoidance, we can begin to relate to difficult thoughts, feelings, sensations, memories, and images like a caring parent soothing a distressed, emotionally dysregulated child. We can be comforting, kind, and compassionate. We can try to understand the pain, not flee from it.

For Christian trauma survivors, we are by no means left alone to lovingly accept our inner world. Instead, God is with us. Because his loving care extends to all of creation, whether our outer world or inner world, we can trust in and surrender to his providence. This brings added comfort, beyond simply accepting inner struggles because avoidance doesn't work. We can begin to ask God what he is up to within our inner world. How is he moving in and through our most difficult thoughts, feelings, and memories? What is he revealing to us in these moments of pain? By recognizing that God is dwelling within, we can begin to relate to our inner world with greater compassion and care. Because God is loving us and consoling us in our pain, we can extend this loving acceptance to ourselves. Since God is working all things out for good, we can trust in his plan. Instead of ruminating with endless "Why" and "What if" questions, we can find a deeper peace in trusting that an infinitely loving, wise, powerful, and present God is actively and purposefully governing. Whether this relates to our outer world or inner world, we have a trustworthy traveling companion. Let's now turn to a self-monitoring activity, followed by the daily examen.

Exercises

Self-Monitoring Log

To begin the exercises in this chapter, please spend a day logging your experiences of intrusive memories, distressing emotions, unhelpful rumination, and efforts to accept your inner world (see Table 8.1). Like the previous three

TABLE 8.1
Self-Monitoring Log

	Intrusive Memories/ Images/ Dreams	Distressing Emotions (Fear, Anxiety, Sadness, Anger, Guilt, Shame, Helplessness, Other)	Type of Unhelpful Rumination ("Why" Questions, "What If" Questions, Meaning of Event, Antecedents or Consequences of Event, Future Events)	Coping Strategy to Accept Your Inner World (Journaling, Praying, Spending Time in Solitude and Silence with God)/Level of Success
6:00 a.m.	*Nightmare of a near-death experience at work.*	*Anxiety and fear.*	*What if I die at work?*	*Trying to surrender my anxiety to God through prayer/ mildly successful.*
7:00 a.m.				
8:00 a.m.				
9:00 a.m.				
10:00 a.m.				
11:00 a.m.				
12:00 p.m.				
1:00 p.m.				
2:00 p.m.				
3:00 p.m.				
4:00 p.m.				
5:00 p.m.				
6:00 p.m.				
7:00 p.m.				
8:00 p.m.				
9:00 p.m.				
10:00 p.m.				
11:00 p.m.				

chapters, this will give you a better sense of your current functioning. It will help you better understand when these trauma symptoms occur throughout the day, how you attempt to cope with them by accepting (not avoiding) them, and your level of success in doing so as you continue with the chapter's activities. I've added an example in the 6:00 a.m. row to get you started. Please use extra paper if needed.

Like the last three chapters, once you have recorded your answers for a day, please respond to the below questions as best you can. Please use extra paper if needed.

1. What relationship, if any, emerged between your possible intrusive memories, distressing emotions, unhelpful ruminations, and coping strategies/level of success? Did you notice a certain pattern that materialized?

_____

_____

_____

_____

_____

_____

2. What types of rumination, if any, did you struggle with in response to possible intrusive memories and distressing emotions?

_____

_____

_____

_____

_____

_____

3. How, if at all, did you attempt to accept (not avoid) your inner world? Were you successful? Why or why not?

_____

_____

_____

_____

_____

_____

Like the last three chapters, the goal is to begin to increase your self-awareness of the relationship between intrusive memories, distressing emotions, rumination, and coping strategies (this time focusing on acceptance, not avoidance, of the inner world). This burgeoning awareness can help you prepare for a different, more intentional strategy—practicing the daily examen. Let's turn now to a spiritual exercise that comes from the Jesuit Christian tradition.

Developing Christian Acceptance with the Daily Examen[47]

In this last chapter of the workbook, you will practice the below steps of the daily examen. You will move toward greater acceptance and an attitude of surrendering consent in the process. You are consenting to God's loving activity, "Finding God in all things." Find a quiet place that is free from distractions, place your smart phone/tablet on silent mode, and meditate for the full 10 minutes. If you are comfortable, close your eyes. Sit up straight in a supportive chair. You can also follow along with the audio file if you'd like: www.routledge.com/9781041088608.

1. Connect with God as you get started. Ask God to reveal himself to you in this 10-minute practice. Ask him to help you see that he is active and present in this very moment. Thank him for his perfect love, which endures forever.
2. Begin to review the day. Ask God for his grace as you reflect on what has occurred in the last several hours. Pray that he will reveal himself to you in all of today's struggles. Ask him to help you see his providential care throughout the day.

3. Ask God to show you how, over the last several hours, he has been present during your trauma-related suffering:
   - ❏ Fears: What am I afraid of? What am I predicting? What are you revealing to me in this difficult experience, God?
   - ❏ Attachments: What am I clinging to? What am I afraid of surrendering? What are you revealing to me in this difficult experience, God?
   - ❏ Control: What am I trying to control? What am I scared of losing? What are you revealing to me in this difficult experience, God?
   - ❏ Entitlements: What do I believe I am entitled to? What am I demanding? What are you revealing to me in this difficult experience, God?

4. Fully and without reservation surrender these four areas—fears, attachments, control, and entitlements—to God. Ask him to take control of them and do what he wishes with them. Ask him to help you accept and trust in his perfect plan for your life.

5. Look out into the future. Continue to surrender your fears, attachments, control, and entitlements to God. Place your hope in his providential care.

6. Conclude the daily examen by praying the following famous prayer from Ignatius of Loyola:

Take, Lord, and receive all my liberty, my memory, my understanding, and my entire will, All I have and call my own. You have given all to me. To you, Lord, I return it. Everything is yours; do with it what you will. Give me only your love and your grace, that is enough for me.[48]

Upon conclusion of the 10-minute practice, try to journal for a few minutes about your experience with the below questions (please use extra paper if needed):

1. What was it like to practice the daily examine to accept your inner world?

_____

_____

_____

_____

_____

_____

2. How well were you able to accept your inner world as you took each step?

_____

_____

_____

_____

_____

_____

3. What was it like to accept, not avoid, your trauma symptoms?

_____

_____

_____

_____

_____

4. How well did practicing the daily examen help you shift from intrusive memories, distressing emotions, and/or trauma-based rumination if these experiences emerged?

_____

_____

_____

_____

_____

5. How can you set aside time to practice the daily examen in daily life?

_____

_____

_____

_____

_____

_____

Remember that you can practice the daily examen every day. Upon doing so, you are learning to accept your trauma symptoms, rather than getting stuck in cycles of trauma-based rumination. With this loving acceptance, you are inviting God to reveal himself, including his providential care, to you amid your inner struggles. Let's now turn to a case example to see the daily examen in action prior to concluding both the chapter and workbook.

Case Example

Leah grew up in a rough neighborhood. Her house was regularly burglarized, and she often went to bed to the sound of gunshots, sirens, and helicopters in the background. She never knew her father, and her mother was in and out of rehabilitation centers due to drug addiction. She had one older brother, Andre, who was aggressive and abusive toward her on an almost daily basis.

Her family lived in a small one-bedroom apartment, and Leah had to share a corner of the living room with Andre as their bedroom. Most days, he would verbally abuse her with insults and derogatory names. Growing up, she felt unlovable and worthless. She also struggled with extreme fear and anxiety because she never knew when Andre would become violent again.

On one afternoon after middle school, Andre accused Leah of eating one of his candy bars. Although she had no recollection of doing so, he insisted she ate it. This led to Andre shoving and hitting Leah. After the violent assault, Leah not only felt the pain of a swollen face, but also the intense fear and anxiety that it would happen again. She also felt an overwhelming sense of powerlessness because her mother wasn't there to protect her.

Although her mother wasn't actively religious, she did raise Leah and Andre with some Baptist teachings sprinkled on top of a mostly secular worldview. Leah recalled that her mother would sometimes sing old church hymns, including the famous song, "It Is Well With My Soul." On occasion, her mother would encourage her to have hope in God when times were rough because he would make things right in the end. Leah internalized these occasional conversations. She truly wanted to trust in God. Still, she struggled to understand why God had placed her in such a violent home with an unrelenting older brother.

After high school, Leah moved away to an out-of-state university. She quickly excelled in school, and she eventually graduated with honors with a bachelor's degree in psychology. Going on to graduate school, she trained to be a social worker to help other people to attain the necessary resources—financial and psychological—to succeed in life.

Yet, even with these academic and professional successes, she still struggled with intrusive memories of her brother's verbal and physical aggression in her adult years. These memories were so vivid that she felt like she was being insulted and hit all over again. Along with these overwhelming images, she felt a combination of fear and shame. She felt fear because she experienced the danger all over again whenever an image or memory would arise. And she felt shame because, deep down, she concluded she was unlovable, ugly, and useless.

Leah also struggled in her relationship with God. In response to the unwanted memories and difficult emotions, she often cried out to God. She would ask God, "Why didn't you protect me from him?" and "What if I'm abused again?" In her efforts to avoid the intrusive images and feelings, she tried to think her way out of the distress. Still, during these moments of rumination, she ended up feeling mentally exhausted. She rarely, if ever, came up with good answers to these pressing questions. Instead, the rumination led to distraction and further fear and shame. And she never felt like she processed what happened and what she truly felt about it.

Fed up with these trauma symptoms, she decided to see a licensed social worker to help her with her ongoing suffering. Down the street from her house, she made an appointment to see Theo. Like Leah, Theo became a social worker to help others. He grew up in a difficult neighborhood, too, and had compassion for those stuck in cycles of poverty, violence, and trauma.

Theo was a committed Christian and explicit about his Christian faith on his professional website. Not only did he have a license to practice clinical social work, but he also had some seminary training. Specifically, he completed coursework in spiritual formation, which provided him with spiritual practices in the Christian tradition to help his Christian clients deepen their relationship with Jesus Christ in a culturally sensitive manner. This was especially important for Leah, given she wanted to approach her trauma from a faith-based perspective. Entering the first counseling session, Leah was both afraid and excited about the possible change that was about to come.

After a session or two to build some safety and trust, Theo and Leah began to address the trauma symptoms she was struggling with. Theo explained that newer theory and research in secular clinical psychology suggests that rumination is often used as a strategy to avoid the unwanted memories and emotions we experience after a traumatic event.[49] Theo went on to suggest that, although rumination may seem like it works, it can often leave trauma survivors stuck in endless cycles of perseverative rumination that distract them from life. And this kind of rumination, Theo stated, can also make trauma symptoms worse.

For Leah, this was the first time that she started to consider that overthinking her trauma may not be the answer. She was also open to an alternative to avoidance. This was especially the case because avoidance had not worked in her adult years. Rather, avoidance left her feeling a deep sense of discouragement. And it prevented her from living her life to the fullest.

Drawing on his training in both mindfulness-based interventions in graduate school and spiritual formation in seminary, Theo proposed an alternative to rumination and avoidance. He suggested that Leah could begin to invite God to be with her in her psychological pain. Theo explained that, through loving acceptance of her memories and emotions, she could learn to engage with life more fully.

About six sessions into her treatment with Theo, Leah and Theo practiced the daily examen. With this practice, Theo suggested, Leah could learn to "Find God in all things," even her trauma symptoms. Although Leah still wanted her trauma symptoms to go away, she began to consider that God was with her in them. And God may be revealing something in and through them. This was a huge shift in perspective for Leah, since she had previously only wanted her symptoms to go away, but to no avail.

As they practiced the daily examen in the sixth session, Theo asked Leah to reflect on her day. He asked her to try to imagine that God was with her in her fear and shame. "What is God revealing to you, Leah?" Theo asked. For possibly the first time, Leah imagined God with her in her fear and shame.

God was revealing himself in her relationship with him. He was helping her to see that he was there to console her in her fear. He was present to offer his love in response to her shame. He was there to love and accept her and make everything okay, something her mother and brother never did growing up. Rather than ruminating on "Why" and "What if" questions about her childhood abuse, she could lovingly accept her fear and shame because God was there to comfort her. This, for Leah, was a huge shift. Rather than trying to ruminate to avoid her fear and shame, she could see God with her. Her fear and shame were reminders that God was with her to console her. Her vivid memories, too, were less overwhelming when she imagined that God was with her. She was no longer alone in them, which may have been the hardest part of the abuse. Rather, she now had a protector and comforter in God. He was there to bring loving comfort when the images and emotions were difficult to endure. He was there in the pain.

Although she would continue to struggle with some trauma symptoms, the daily examen helped her to see God in her suffering. He was working her life out for good. He was the benevolent king, and she was an active participant in his kingdom. He was actively and purposefully guiding her life all along, even if she didn't have all the "Why" questions sorted out. Instead of getting stuck in ruminative doubt, she could trust in God's providence.

Conclusion

In this concluding chapter, we explored the role that loving acceptance can play in responding to trauma symptoms with kindness and openness. Rather than trying to avoid our symptoms with rumination, we can learn to relate differently to intrusive memories and distressing emotions. Like a comforting, nurturing parent, we can try to understand our suffering and respond to it with care. And this loving acceptance can be employed for pragmatic reasons—because avoidance doesn't work, and rumination doesn't work to avoid trauma symptoms. We are, from this perspective, taking what is offered.[50] We are recognizing that, anchored to reality, our trauma symptoms may never go away. However, we can learn to be more nurturing and kinder to what is already there. We don't have to be aggressive or shaming toward our inner experiences.

Yet, for many Christian trauma survivors, loving acceptance needs to be housed within our own faith tradition, not Buddhist mindfulness as the vehicle for change. And God's providence means that we can move beyond simply accepting for merely pragmatic reasons. Instead, we can accept our inner world with love, kindness, gentleness, and openness because God is purposefully and actively working everything out for good, even our inner experiences. Because God is infinitely loving, wise, powerful, and present, he knows what is best for us, knows all possible outcomes, has the power to carry out the best possible outcome, and is present with us as he carries out his perfect plan. This God of the Bible is a personal God who cares for the big and small of his creation and everything in between. He is a God who cares for both our outer world and inner world. Because of this, we can accept, not fight against via avoidance, our inner world with more affection and a nurturing posture.

My hope is that this workbook has helped you recognize your trauma-based rumination and gently and lovingly shift toward God. God offers us his deeper peace from moment to moment. He does so by dwelling within. He also does so by guiding the world we walk with him in. With each step we take in life, we come to a mental fork in the road. We do not need to travel alone down the road of unhelpful rumination. Instead, we can recognize that God is dwelling within. We can travel with him down the road of helpful rumination. Through the Christian skills of attention, focus on the present moment, awareness, and acceptance, we can learn to walk with him more confidently and recognize his loving presence. If Christian mental health is simply defined as being empowered by the Holy Spirit to walk with the Son home to the outstretched arms of the Father, my prayer is that this four-skill approach has helped you to do so.

To end this workbook, I leave you with a famous prayer attributed to the Christian reformer Martin Luther:

> Behold, Lord, I am an empty vessel that needs to be filled. O Lord, fill me. I am weak in the faith; strengthen me. I am cold in love; warm me to the point of zeal so that my love may reach my neighbor. I do not have a steadfast belief. I suffer from doubt, and I am unable to trust completely. O Lord, help me. Increase my faith and strengthen my trust. All my good treasure is stored in you.[51]

At the end of the day, the Christian life is about recognizing that we are finite and dependent, and God is infinite and independent. Yet, he chose to take on human form to reconcile us to him because he loves us. Instead of being distant and apathetic, he lovingly cares for his creation, even though he may not reveal to us all the answers when it comes to trauma. Although we can certainly lament to God with "Why" questions, we need to learn to gently pivot toward his loving presence when we get stuck. We need to shift from a causal to functional view of suffering.[52] We need to embrace our worldview, which need not be completely shattered.[53] Although traumatic events may leave us feeling broken and in pieces, God is our bonding agent. He glues us back together as our Maker. I wholeheartedly believe that, although certainly scary, we need to surrender to the love of God, fully and totally, as the Christian response to trauma symptoms. I can personally attest to this in my own arduous journey as a trauma survivor. We can do so not merely for pragmatic, practical reasons—because avoidance doesn't work—but also because we follow, worship, and serve an infinitely good, wise, powerful, and present Creator, Sustainer, and Redeemer who holds all things together.[54]

Notes

1 APA Dictionary (n.d.a).
2 Harris (2019).
3 Hayes et al. (2012).
4 Gámez et al. (2011).
5 Lewis and Naugle (2017).
6 Bishop et al. (2018).
7 Bishop et al. (2018).
8 Ehlers and Clark (2000).
9 Hayes (2019).
10 Siegel (2022).

11 Siegel (2022).
12 Shapiro (2020).
13 Shapiro (2020).
14 Shapiro (2020).
15 Siegel (2009).
16 Germer (2009).
17 Germer (2009).
18 Michael et al. (2007).
19 Hayes (2019); Segal et al. (2012).
20 Segal et al. (2012).
21 Bishop et al. (2018).
22 Ehlers and Clark (2000).
23 Holman Bible Dictionary (2004b).
24 Holman Bible Dictionary (2004b); Piper (2020).
25 Romans 8:28.
26 Flavel (2022).
27 Colombiere (1980).
28 Genesis 50:20.
29 Romans 8:28.
30 Philippians 4:11–13.
31 Protestant Reformed Churches in America (n.d.).
32 Michael et al. (2007).
33 Ehlers and Clark (2000).
34 Michael et al. (2007).
35 Segal et al. (2012).
36 Colombiere (1980).
37 Colombiere (1980).
38 Matthew 6:25–27.
39 Colombiere (1980).
40 Ignatian Spirituality (n.d.a).
41 Ignatian Spirituality (n.d.a).
42 McMartin and Hall (2022).
43 Thibodeaux (2015).
44 Knabb et al. (2022).
45 Knabb et al. (2017).
46 Michael et al. (2007).
47 This six-step daily examen is based on a review of Ignatian Spirituality (n.d.a), Thibodeaux (2015), Colombiere (1980), and Aschenbrenner (2007), with portions from Knabb et al. (2019c).
48 Loyola Press (n.d.).
49 Ehlers and Clark (2000); Michael et al. (2007).
50 Hayes et al. (2012).
51 Arnold and Carter (2024, p. 69).
52 McMartin and Hall (2022).
53 Janoff-Bulman (1992).
54 Colossians 1:17.

References

American Psychiatric Association. (2022). *Diagnostic and statistical manual of mental disorders* (5th ed., text rev.). https://doi.org/10.1176/appi.books.9780890425787

Anderson, T., Clark, W., & Naugle, D. (2017). *An introduction to Christian worldview: Pursuing God's perspective in a pluralistic world.* IVP Academic.

APA Dictionary. (n.d.a). 'Acceptance'. https://dictionary.apa.org/acceptance

APA Dictionary. (n.d.b). 'Attention'. https://dictionary.apa.org/attention

APA Dictionary. (n.d.c). 'Awareness'. https://dictionary.apa.org/awareness

APA Dictionary. (n.d.d). 'Compassion'. https://dictionary.apa.org/compassion

APA Dictionary. (n.d.e). 'Rumination'. https://dictionary.apa.org/rumination

APA Dictionary. (n.d.f). 'Trauma'. https://dictionary.apa.org/trauma

Arnold, J., & Carter, Z. (Eds.). (2024). *Cloud of witnesses: A treasury of prayers and petitions through the ages.* Crossway.

Aschenbrenner, G. (2007). *Examen.* British Province of the Society of Jesus.

Atwoli, L., Stein, D. J., Koenen, K. C., & McLaughlin, K. A. (2015). Epidemiology of posttraumatic stress disorder: Prevalence, correlates and consequences. *Current Opinion in Psychiatry, 28*(4), 307–311. https://doi.org/10.1097/YCO.0000000000000167

Ball, J. (2016). *A treatise of divine meditation.* Puritan Publications.

Barclay, W. (1974). *New Testament words.* Westminster John Knox Press.

Beasley-Topliffe, K. (Ed.). (2003). *The upper room dictionary of Christian spiritual formation.* Upper Room Books.

Beck, J. (2021). *Cognitive therapy: Basics and beyond* (3rd ed.). Guilford Press.

Beeke, J. (2016). *How can I practice Christian meditation?* Reformation Heritage Books.

Beeke, J., & Jones, M. (2012). *A Puritan theology: Doctrine for life.* Reformation Heritage Books.

Beeke, J., & La Belle, J. (2010). *Living by God's promises.* Reformation Heritage Books.

Benjet, C., Bromet, E., Karam, E. G., Kessler, R. C., McLaughlin, K. A., Ruscio, A. M., & Koenen, K. C. (2016). The epidemiology of traumatic event exposure worldwide: Results from the World Mental Health Survey Consortium. *Psychological Medicine, 46*(2), 327–343. https://doi.org/10.1017/S0033291715001981

Bible Hub. (n.d.). *Eleos.* https://biblehub.com/greek/1656.htm

Birrer, E., & Michael, T. (2011). Rumination in PTSD as well as in traumatized and non-traumatized depressed patients: A cross-sectional clinical study. *Behavioural and Cognitive Psychotherapy, 39*(4), 381–397. https://doi.org/10.1017/S1352465811000087

Bishop, L. S., Ameral, V. E., & Palm Reed, K. M. (2018). The impact of experiential avoidance and event centrality in trauma-related rumination and posttraumatic stress. *Behavior Modification, 42*(6), 815–837. https://doi.org/10.1177/0145445517747287

Bishop, S. R., Lau, M., Shapiro, S., Carlson, L., Anderson, N. D., Carmody, J., … & Devins, G. (2004). Mindfulness: A proposed operational definition. *Clinical Psychology: Science and Practice, 11*(3), 230.

Bourgeault, C. (2004). *Centering prayer and inner awakening.* Cowley Publications.

Briere, J. (2015). Pain and suffering: A synthesis of Buddhist and Western approaches to trauma. In V. Follette, J. Briere, D. Rozelle, J. Hopper, & D. Rome (Eds.), *Mindfulness-oriented interventions for trauma: Integrating contemplative practices* (pp. 11–30). Guilford Press.

Brueggemann, W. (1985). *The message of the Psalms.* Fortress Press.

Byfield, N. (2013). *The promises of God.* Puritan Publications.

Cann, A., Calhoun, L. G., Tedeschi, R. G., Triplett, K. N., Vishnevsky, T., & Lindstrom, C. M. (2011). Assessing posttraumatic cognitive processes: The event related rumination inventory. *Anxiety, Stress, & Coping, 24*(2), 137–156. https://doi.org/10.1080/10615806.2010.529901

Chang, V., Scott, S., & Decker, C. (2013). *Developing helping skills: A step-by-step approach.* Cengage.

Clohessy, S., & Ehlers, A. (1999). PTSD symptoms, response to intrusive memories, and coping in ambulance service workers. *British Journal of Clinical Psychology, 38,* 251–265. https://doi.org/10.1348/014466599162836

Colombiere, C. (1980). *Trustful surrender to divine providence: The secret of peace and happiness.* Tan Books.

Coniaris, A. (1998). *Philokalia: The Bible of Orthodox spirituality* [Kindle version]. Light & Life Publishing Company.

Crane, R. (2009). *Mindfulness-based cognitive therapy.* Routledge.

Dickson, K. S., Ciesla, J. A., & Reilly, L. C. (2012). Rumination, worry, cognitive avoidance, and behavioral avoidance: Examination of temporal effects. *Behavior Therapy*, *43*(3), 629–640. https://doi.org/10.1016/j.beth.2011.11.002

Dube, S. R., Anda, R. F., Felitti, V. J., Chapman, D. P., Williamson, D. F., & Giles, W. H. (2001). Childhood abuse, household dysfunction, and the risk of attempted suicide throughout the life span: Findings from the Adverse Childhood Experiences Study. *JAMA*, *286*(24), 3089–3096. https://doi.org/10.1001/jama.286.24.3089

Ehlers, A., & Clark, D. (2000). A cognitive model of posttraumatic stress disorder. *Behaviour Research and Therapy*, *38*, 319–345. https://doi.org/10.1016/S0005-7967(99)00123-0

Ehlers, A., & Steil, R. (1995). Maintenance of intrusive memories in posttraumatic stress disorder: A cognitive approach. *Behavioural and Cognitive Psychotherapy*, *23*, 217–249. https://doi.org/10.1017/S135246580001585X

Ehring, T., & Ehlers, A. (2014). Does rumination mediate the relationship between emotion regulation ability and posttraumatic stress disorder? *European Journal of Psychotraumatology*, *5*, 1–7. https://doi.org/10.3402/ejpt.v5.23547

Ehring, T., Szeimies, A. K., & Schaffrick, C. (2009). An experimental analogue study into the role of abstract thinking in trauma-related rumination. *Behaviour Research and Therapy*, *47*(4), 285–293. https://doi.org/10.1016/j.brat.2008.12.011

Elwell, W. (Ed.). (2001). *Evangelical dictionary of theology* (Rev. ed.). Baker Academic.

Feldman, G., Hayes, A., Kumar, S., Greeson, J., & Laurenceau, J. (2007). Mindfulness and emotion regulation: The development and initial validation of the cognitive and affective mindfulness scale-revised (CAMS-R). *Journal of Psychopathology and Behavioral Assessment*, *29*, 177–190. https://doi.org/10.1007/s10862-006-9035-8

Felitti, V. J., Anda, R. F., Nordenberg, D., Williamson, D. F., Spitz, A. M., Edwards, V., & Marks, J. S. (1998). Relationship of childhood abuse and household dysfunction to many of the leading causes of death in adults: The Adverse Childhood Experiences (ACE) Study. *American Journal of Preventive Medicine*, *14*(4), 245–258. https://doi.org/10.1016/S0749-3797(98)00017-8

Flavel, J. (2022). *The mystery of providence*. Banner of Truth Trust.

Follette, V., & Pistorello, J. (2007). *Finding life beyond trauma: Using acceptance and commitment therapy to heal from post-traumatic stress and trauma-related problems*. New Harbinger.

Follette, V., Palm, K. M., & Pearson, A. N. (2006). Mindfulness and trauma: Implications for treatment. *Journal of Rational-Emotive and*

Cognitive-Behavior Therapy, 24, 45–61. https://doi.org/10.1007/s10
942-006-0025-2

Foster, R. (2001). *Streams of living water: Celebrating the great traditions of Christian faith.* HarperOne.

Frewen, P., Zhu, J., & Lanius, R. (2019). Lifetime traumatic stressors and adverse childhood experiences uniquely predict concurrent PTSD, complex PTSD, and dissociative subtype of PTSD symptoms whereas recent adult non-traumatic stressors do not: Results from an online survey study. *European Journal of Psychotraumatology, 10*(1), 1606625. https://doi.org/10.1080/20008198.2019.1606625

Gallagher, T. (2006). *The examen prayer: Ignatian wisdom for our lives today.* The Crossroad Publishing Company.

Gámez, W., Chmielewski, M., Kotov, R., Ruggero, C., & Watson, D. (2011). Development of a measure of experiential avoidance: The Multidimensional Experiential Avoidance Questionnaire. *Psychological Assessment, 23*(3), 692. https://doi.org/10.1037/a0023242

García, F. E., Duque, A., & Cova, F. (2017). The four faces of rumination to stressful events: A psychometric analysis. *Psychological Trauma: Theory, Research, Practice, and Policy, 9*(6), 758. https://doi.org/10.1037/tra0000289

Germer, C. (2009). *The mindful path to self-compassion: Freeing yourself from destructive thoughts and emotions.* Guilford Press.

Germer, C., & Neff, K. (2015). Cultivating self-compassion in trauma survivors. In V. Follette, J. Briere, D. Rozelle, J. Hopper, & D. Rome (Eds.), *Mindfulness-oriented interventions for trauma: Integrating contemplative practices.* Guilford Press.

Germer, C., & Neff, K. (2018). *The mindful self-compassion workbook: A proven way to accept yourself, build inner strength, and thrive.* Guilford Press.

Gilbert, P. (2010). *Compassion-focused therapy.* Routledge.

Gluhoski, V. L., & Wortman, C. B. (1996). The impact of trauma on world views. *Journal of Social and Clinical Psychology, 15*(4), 417–429. https://doi.org/10.1521/jscp.1996.15.4.417

Goggin, J., & Strobel, K. (Ed.). (2013). *Reading the Christian spiritual classics: A guide for Evangelicals.* InterVarsity Press.

Hall, M. E. L., & Hill, P. (2019). Meaning-making, suffering, and religion: A worldview conception. *Mental Health, Religion & Culture, 22*(5), 467–479. https://doi.org/10.1080/13674676.2019.1625037

Harris, R. (2019). *ACT made simple: An easy-to-read primer on acceptance and commitment therapy* (2nd ed.). New Harbinger Publications.

Hawley, L. L., Schwartz, D., Bieling, P. J., Irving, J., Corcoran, K., Farb, N. A., & Segal, Z. V. (2014). Mindfulness practice, rumination and clinical outcome in mindfulness-based treatment. *Cognitive Therapy and Research, 38*, 1–9. https://doi.org/10.1007/s10608-013-9586-4

Hayes, S. (2019). *A liberated mind: How to pivot toward what matters.* Avery.

Hayes, S., Follette, V., & Linehan, M. (Eds.). (2011). *Mindfulness and acceptance: Expanding the cognitive behavioral tradition.* Guilford Press.

Hayes, S., Strosahl, K., & Wilson, K. (2012). *Acceptance and commitment therapy: The process and practice of mindful change* (2nd ed.). Guilford Press.

Heyman, G. (2007). *The power of sacrifice: Roman & Christian discourses in conflict.* The Catholic University of America Press.

Holman Bible Dictionary. (2004a). *Meditation.* Holman Bible Publishers.

Holman Bible Dictionary. (2004b). *Providence.* Holman Bible Publishers.

Hopwood, T. L., & Schutte, N. S. (2017). A meta-analytic investigation of the impact of mindfulness-based interventions on posttraumatic stress. *Clinical Psychology Review, 57*, 12–20. https://doi.org/10.1016/j.cpr.2017.08.002

Ignatian Spirituality. (n.d.a). *The daily examen.* www.ignatianspirituality.com/ignatian-prayer/the-examen

Ignatian Spirituality. (n.d.b). *What are the spiritual exercises?* www.ignatianspirituality.com/ignatian-prayer/the-spiritual-exercises/what-are-the-spiritual-exercises

Im, S., & Follette, V. M. (2016). Rumination and mindfulness related to multiple types of trauma exposure. *Translational Issues in Psychological Science, 2*(4), 395. https://psycnet.apa.org/doi/10.1037/tps0000090

Ivens, M. (1998). *Understanding the spiritual exercises: Text and commentary: A handbook for retreat directors.* Cromwell Press.

Janoff-Bulman, R. (1992). *Shattered assumptions: Towards a new psychology of trauma.* The Free Press.

Junnarkar, M., & Lakhani, S. (2021). Investigating the eyewitness: Accuracy and fallacies of memory. In S. Sahni & P. Bhadra (Eds.), *Criminal psychology and the criminal justice system in India and beyond* (pp. 203–214). Springer.

Keator, M. (2018). *Lectio divina as contemplative pedagogy: Re-appropriating monastic practice for the humanities.* Routledge.

Kessler, R. C., Aguilar-Gaxiola, S., Alonso, J., Benjet, C., Bromet, E. J., Cardoso, G., & Koenen, K. C. (2017). Trauma and PTSD in the WHO world mental health surveys. *European Journal of Psychotraumatology, 8*(sup5), 1353383. https://doi.org/10.1080/20008198.2017.1353383

Knabb, J. J. (2021). *Christian meditation in clinical practice: A four-step model and workbook for therapist and clients.* IVP Academic.

Knabb, J. J. (2022). *Acceptance and commitment therapy for Christian clients: A faith-based workbook* (2nd ed.). Routledge.

Knabb, J. J., & Vazquez, V. E. (2018). A randomized controlled trial of a 2-week internet-based contemplative prayer program for Christians with daily stress. *Spirituality in Clinical Practice, 5*(1), 37–53. https://doi.org/10.1037/scp0000154

Knabb, J. J., & Vazquez, V. E. (2025). Decentering mindfulness: Toward greater meditative diversity in global public health. *Mindfulness, 16*, 647–654. https://doi.org/10.1007/s12671-023-02203-7

Knabb, J. J., & Wang, K. T. (2021). The Communion with God Scale: Shifting from an etic to emic perspective to assess fellowshipping with the Triune God. *Psychology of Religion and Spirituality, 13*(1), 67. https://psycnet.apa.org/doi/10.1037/rel0000272

Knabb, J. J., Frederick, T. V., & Cumming III, G. (2017). Surrendering to god's providence: A three-part study on providence-focused therapy for recurrent worry (PFT-RW). *Psychology of Religion and Spirituality, 9*(2), 180. https://doi.org/10.1037/rel0000081

Knabb, J. J., Johnson, E., Bates, T., & Sisemore, T. (2019b). *Christian psychotherapy in context: Theoretical and empirical explorations in faith-based mental health.* Routledge.

Knabb, J. J., Vazquez, V., & Pate, R. (2019a). "Set your minds on things above": Shifting from trauma-based ruminations to ruminating on God. *Mental Health, Religion & Culture, 22*(4), 384–399. https://doi.org/10.1080/13674676.2019.1612336

Knabb, J. J., Vazquez, V. E., Pate, R., Garzon, F. L., & Wang, K. T. (2019c). *Christian meditation for trauma-based rumination: A four-week program.* Unpublished manual.

Knabb, J. J., Vazquez, V. E., Pate, R. A., Garzon, F. L., Wang, K. T., Edison-Riley, D., Slick, A. R., Smith, R. R., & Weber, S. E. (2022). Christian meditation for trauma-based rumination: A two-part study examining the effects of an internet-based 4-week program. *Spirituality in Clinical Practice, 9*(4), 253–271. https://doi.org/10.1037/scp0000255

Knabb, J. J., Vazquez, V. E., & Wang, K. T. (2021). The Christian Contentment Scale: An emic measure for assessing inner satisfaction within the Christian tradition. *Journal of Psychology and Theology, 49*(4), 324–341. https://doi.org/10.1177/0091647120968146

Knabb, J. J., Wang, K. T., Hall, M. E. L., & Vazquez, V. E. (2025). The Christian Worldview Scale: An emic measure for assessing a comprehensive view of life within the Christian tradition. *Spirituality in Clinical Practice, 12*(1), 1–19. https://doi.org/10.1037/scp0000306

Lawrence, B. (2015). *The practice of the presence of God.* (S. Sciurba, Trans.). ICS Publications.

Leahy, R. (2017). *Cognitive therapy techniques: A practitioner's guide* (2nd ed.). Guilford Press.

Leigh, E., Taylor, L., Cole, V., & Smith, P. (2025). Why is rumination unhelpful in adolescents? Two studies examining the causal role of abstract processing. *Journal of Affective Disorders*. https://doi.org/10.1016/j.jad.2025.03.058

Lewis, M., & Naugle, A. (2017). Measuring experiential avoidance: Evidence toward multidimensional predictors of trauma sequelae. *Behavioral Sciences, 7*(1), 9. https://doi.org/10.3390/bs7010009

Lewis, C., Roberts, N. P., Andrew, M., Starling, E., & Bisson, J. I. (2020). Psychological therapies for post-traumatic stress disorder in adults: Systematic review and meta-analysis. *European Journal of Psychotraumatology, 11*(1), 1729633. https://doi.org/10.1080/20008198.2020.1729633

Loyola Press. (n.d.). *Suscipe*. www.loyolapress.com/our-catholic-faith/prayer/traditional-catholic-prayers/saints-prayers/suscipe-prayer-saint-ignatius-of-loyola

Lutz, A., Slagter, H. A., Dunne, J. D., & Davidson, R. J. (2008). Attention regulation and monitoring in meditation. *Trends in Cognitive Sciences, 12*(4), 163–169. https://doi.org/10.1016/j.tics.2008.01.005

Mao, L., Li, P., Wu, Y., Luo, L., & Hu, M. (2023). The effectiveness of mindfulness-based interventions for ruminative thinking: A systematic review and meta-analysis of randomized controlled trials. *Journal of Affective Disorders, 321*, 83–95. https://doi.org/10.1016/j.jad.2022.10.022

McLean, C. P., Levy, H. C., Miller, M. L., & Tolin, D. F. (2022). Exposure therapy for PTSD: A meta-analysis. *Clinical Psychology Review, 91*, 102115. https://doi.org/10.1016/j.cpr.2021.102115

McMartin, J., & Hall, M. E. L. (2022). Christian functional views of suffering: A review and theoretical overview. *Mental Health, Religion & Culture, 25*(3), 247–262. https://doi.org/10.1080/13674676.2021.1968812

Merriam-Webster. (n.d.). *Rumination*. Merriam-Webster Dictionary. www.merriam-webster.com/medical/rumination

Michael, T., Halligan, S., Clark, D., & Ehlers, A. (2007). Rumination in post-traumatic stress disorder. *Depression and Anxiety, 24*, 307–317. https://doi.org/10.1002/da.20228

Middleton, P. (2011). *Martyrdom: A guide for the perplexed*. T&T Clark International.

Miethe, S., Wigger, J., Wartemann, A., Fuchs, F. O., & Trautmann, S. (2023). Posttraumatic stress symptoms and its association with rumination, thought suppression and experiential avoidance: A systematic review and meta-analysis. *Journal of Psychopathology and Behavioral Assessment, 45*(2), 480–495. https://doi.org/10.1007/s10862-023-10022-2

Mills, K. L., McFarlane, A. C., Slade, T., Creamer, M., Silove, D., Teesson, M., & Bryant, R. (2011). Assessing the prevalence of trauma exposure in epidemiological surveys. *Australian & New Zealand Journal of Psychiatry, 45*(5), 407–415. https://doi.org/10.3109/00048674.2010.543654

Moulds, M. L., Bisby, M. A., Wild, J., & Bryant, R. A. (2020). Rumination in posttraumatic stress disorder: A systematic review. *Clinical Psychology Review, 82*, 101910. https://doi.org/10.1016/j.cpr.2020.101910

Nacasch, N., Rachamim, L., & Foa, E. (2015). Prolonged exposure treatment. In M. Safir, H. Wallach, & A. Rizzo (Eds.), *Future directions in post-traumatic stress disorder: Prevention, diagnosis, and treatment* (pp. 245–252). Springer.

Neff, K. D. (2003). The development and validation of a scale to measure self-compassion. *Self and Identity, 2*(3), 223–250. https://doi.org/10.1080/15298860309027

Nikodimos. (Ed.). (1782). *Philokalia*. R.P. Pryne.

Nitzan-Assayag, Y., Aderka, I. M., & Bernstein, A. (2015). Dispositional mindfulness in trauma recovery: Prospective relations and mediating mechanisms. *Journal of Anxiety Disorders, 36*, 25–32. https://doi.org/10.1016/j.janxdis.2015.07.008

Nolen-Hoeksema, S., Morrow, J., & Fredrickson, B. L. (1993). Response styles and the duration of episodes of depressed mood. *Journal of Abnormal Psychology, 102*(1), 20–28. https://doi.org/10.1037/0021-843X.102.1.20

Oman, D. (2024). What is a mantra? Guidance for practitioners, researchers, and editors. *American Psychologist*. https://doi.org/10.1037/amp0001368

Packer, J. (2009). *Rediscovering holiness: Know the fullness of life with God*. Regal.

Paintner, C. (2012). *Desert fathers and mothers: Early Christian wisdom sayings*. Turner Publishing Company.

Patzia, A. (1990). *Ephesians, Colossians, Philemon*. Baker Books.

Pew Research Center. (2021). *Views on human suffering and God's role in it*. www.pewresearch.org/religion/2021/11/23/views-on-human-suffering-and-gods-role-in-it/#views-on-god-s-role-in-human-suffering

Piper, J. (2020). *Providence*. Crossway.

Protestant Reformed Churches in America. (n.d.). *Belgic confession*. www.prca.org/about/official-standards/creeds/three-forms-of-unity/belgic-confession

Ramos, C., Leal, I., Costa, P. A., Tapadinhas, A. R., & Tedeschi, R. G. (2018). An item-level analysis of the posttraumatic stress disorder checklist and the posttraumatic growth inventory and its associations with challenge to core beliefs and rumination. *Frontiers in Psychology, 9*, 2346. https://doi.org/10.3389/fpsyg.2018.02346

Saint Bernard of Clairvaux. (2016). *Commentary on the Song of Songs*. Jazzybee Verlag.

Santa Maria, A., Reichert, F., Hummel, S. B., & Ehring, T. (2012). Effects of rumination on intrusive memories: Does processing mode matter? *Journal of Behavior Therapy and Experimental Psychiatry, 43*(3), 901–909. https://doi.org/10.1016/j.jbtep.2012.01.004

Schein, J., Houle, C., Urganus, A., Cloutier, M., Patterson-Lomba, O., Wang, Y., & Davis, L. L. (2021). Prevalence of post-traumatic stress disorder in the United States: A systematic literature review. *Current Medical Research and Opinion, 37*(12), 2151–2161. https://doi.org/10.1080/03007 995.2021.1978417

Schuler, E. R., & Boals, A. (2016). Shattering world assumptions: A prospective view of the impact of adverse events on world assumptions. *Psychological Trauma: Theory, Research, Practice, and Policy, 8*(3), 259–266. https://doi. org/10.1037/tra0000073

Segal, Z., Williams, M., & Teasdale, J. (2012). *Mindfulness-based cognitive therapy for depression* (2nd ed.). The Guilford Press.

Shapiro, S. (2020). *Good morning, I love you: Mindfulness and self-compassion practices to rewire your brain for calm, clarity, and joy*. Sounds True.

Siegel, R. (2009). *The mindfulness solution: Everyday practices for everyday problems*. Guilford Press.

Siegel, R. (2022). *The extraordinary gift of being ordinary: Finding happiness right where you are*. Guilford Press.

Spurstowe, W. (2012). *The wells of salvation opened*. Puritan Publications.

Stanford Encyclopedia of Philosophy. (2024). *Theodicies*. https://plato.stanford. edu/entries/theodicies

Steil, R., & Ehlers, A. (2000). Dysfunctional meaning of posttraumatic intrusions in chronic PTSD. *Behaviour Research and Therapy, 38*, 537–558. https://doi.org/10.1016/S0005-7967(99)00069-8

Stroebe, M., Boelen, P. A., Van Den Hout, M., Stroebe, W., Salemink, E., & Van Den Bout, J. (2007). Ruminative coping as avoidance: A reinterpretation of its function in adjustment to bereavement. *European Archives of Psychiatry and Clinical Neuroscience, 257*, 462–472. https://doi.org/10.1007/s00 406-007-0746-y

Strohmaier, S., Jones, F. W., & Cane, J. E. (2021). Effects of length of mindfulness practice on mindfulness, depression, anxiety, and stress: A randomized controlled experiment. *Mindfulness, 12*, 198–214. https://doi.org/10.1007/ s12671-020-01512-5

Talbot, J. (2013). *The Jesus prayer: A cry for mercy, a path of renewal*. InterVarsity Press.

Talbot, J. (2020). *Desert dangers and delights: Stories, teachings, and sources*. Liturgical Press.

Teasdale, J., Williams, J., & Segal, Z. (2014). *The mindful way workbook: An 8-week program to free yourself from depression and emotional distress*. Guilford Press.

Thibodeaux, M. (2015). *Reimagining the Ignatian Examen: Fresh ways to pray from your day*. Loyola Press.

Tirch, D., Silberstein, L., & Kolts, R. (2016). *Buddhist psychology and cognitive behavioral therapy: A clinician's guide.* Guilford Press.

Treier, D. (Ed.). (2017). *Evangelical dictionary of theology* (3rd ed.). Baker Academic.

Vest, N. (2008). *No moment too small: Rhythms of silence, prayer, & holy reading.* Rowan & Littlefield Publishers.

Walser, R. D., & Hayes, S. C. (2006). Acceptance and commitment therapy in the treatment of posttraumatic stress disorder. In V. M. Follette & J. I Ruzek (Eds.), *Cognitive-behavioral therapies for trauma* (pp. 146–172). Guilford Press.

Wang, Y., Fu, C., Liu, Y., Li, D., Wang, C., Sun, R., & Song, Y. (2021). A study on the effects of mindfulness-based cognitive therapy and loving-kindness mediation on depression, rumination, mindfulness level and quality of life in depressed patients. *American Journal of Translational Research, 13*(5), 4666. https://pmc.ncbi.nlm.nih.gov/articles/PMC8205847

Ware, K. (2014). *The Jesus prayer.* Catholic Truth Society.

Watkins, E. R. (2008). Constructive and unconstructive repetitive thought. *Psychological Bulletin, 134*(2), 163–206. https://doi.org/10.1037/0033-2909.134.2.163

Watkins, E. R., & Roberts, H. (2020). Reflecting on rumination: Consequences, causes, mechanisms and treatment of rumination. *Behaviour Research and Therapy, 127*, 103573. https://doi.org/10.1016/j.brat.2020.103573

Wellington, J. (2020). *Journeying with the Jesus prayer.* SLG Press.

Western Shorter Catechism. (1648). https://prts.edu/wp-content/uploads/2016/12/Shorter_Catechism.pdf

Wilt, J., Exline, J., Lindberg, M., Park, C., & Pargament, K. (2017). Theological beliefs about suffering and interactions with the divine. *Psychology of Religion and Spirituality, 9*, 137–147. https://doi.org/10.1037/rel0000067

Winders, S. J., Murphy, O., Looney, K., & O'Reilly, G. (2020). Self-compassion, trauma, and posttraumatic stress disorder: A systematic review. *Clinical Psychology & Psychotherapy, 27*(3), 300–329. https://doi.org/10.1002/cpp.2429

Wright, C. (2006). *The mission of God: Unlocking the Bible's grand narrative.* InterVarsity Press.

Index

For Product Safety Concerns and Information please contact our EU
representative GPSR@taylorandfrancis.com
Taylor & Francis Verlag GmbH, Kaufingerstraße 24, 80331 München, Germany

www.ingramcontent.com/pod-product-compliance
Lightning Source LLC
Chambersburg PA
CBHW080133270326
41926CB00021B/4471

9 781041 088608